THE
RIGHT
BRAIN

Thomas R. Blakeslee

THE RIGHT BRAIN

*A New Understanding
of the Unconscious
Mind and Its
Creative Powers*

ANCHOR PRESS/DOUBLEDAY
GARDEN CITY, NEW YORK

Library of Congress Cataloging in Publication Data

Blakeslee, Thomas R   1937–
  The right brain.

  Bibliography: p. 223.
  Includes index.
  1. Left and right (Psychology)   2. Thought and
thinking.   3. Subconsciousness (Psychology)
4. Creative thinking.   5. Brain.   I. Title.
[DNLM: 1. Dominance, Cerebral.   2. Brain mapping.
WL335 B637r]
BF455.B47   153
ISBN: 0-385-15099-7
Library of Congress Catalog Card Number 79–26209

To Maureen—whose ideas, patience, and hard work made this book possible

CONTENTS

Part I

THE RIGHT-BRAIN REVOLUTION

Chapter 1

YOUR SILENT PARTNER

In this age of computers and space travel, our understanding of our own mind is as erroneous as the ancients' idea of the earth as a flat surface. We have been fooled by a powerful illusion of mental unity into ignoring and misunderstanding the thoughts, knowledge, and emotions of half of our brain. Just as mankind was fooled for centuries by the "obvious" flatness of the earth, we have accepted a false understanding of our minds based on what we seem to see clearly when we look at our own thoughts.

The misconception in both cases results from the fact that we see so clearly only a *part* of the picture: When we look at the terrain around us, the earth looks convincingly flat, yet other less visible evidence proves that the earth is actually a sphere spinning through space. Likewise, when we examine our thoughts, we use a process called introspection to report *in words* what we see. Naturally, a verbal examination of our thoughts will reveal only thoughts that can be expressed in words.

Scientific evidence now indicates that only the left half

of our brain is capable of expressing its thoughts in words. The right side of the brain has its own separate train of thoughts, which are *not* in words. Though these nonverbal thoughts are a crucial part of our personality and abilities, they continue to be ignored and misunderstood because they are so difficult to translate into words.

Since the right side of the brain is capable of controlling our actions, solving problems, remembering things, and having emotions, it fully qualifies as a mind by itself. In spite of this fact, we have continued to look at our mind as a singular entity that thinks only in words. And just as the "flat earth" model produced a number of paradoxes that required mystical explanations, the single-mind model makes the human mind seem much more mysterious than it is.

When you look at a human brain it is difficult to see how people could ever have thought of it as the physical basis of a singular "mind." For the human brain is clearly a *double* organ consisting of *two identical-looking hemispheres* joined together by several bundles of nerve fibers.

If the human mind is really singular, then how could it reside in two places at once? Certainly the billions of neurons in the two hemispheres are not so identical that they can simultaneously conceive identical thoughts on each side. Yet if the human mind resides strictly in one of the hemispheres, what could the equal amount of brain power in the other hemisphere be doing? Evolutionary forces simply do not allow the kind of waste that would be represented by having one hemisphere sit idle. In fact, measurements of the rate of metabolism of the two hemi-

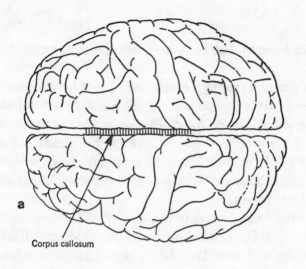

Corpus callosum

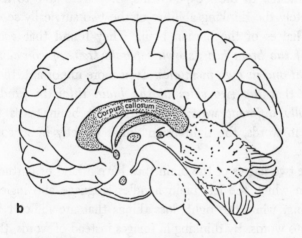

Corpus callosum

1. *The Human Brain*
   (a) Top view of left and right hemispheres (cortex)
   (b) Right hemisphere only as seen from the midline.
   The shaded areas are the neural connections between left and right which are cut in the split-brain operation.

spheres indicate that both are doing the same amount of work.

For almost a century we have known that human powers of speech reside primarily in the left hemisphere:* Injuries on the left side cause speech damage, while right-brain injuries leave speech intact. In spite of this understanding, we have only recently begun to appreciate how the functions of the brain are actually divided between the left and right hemispheres.

The real breakthrough in this understanding came in the 1960s when Dr. Roger Sperry and his students Michael Gazzaniga and Jerre Levy began their historic split-brain experiments. In these experiments, they were able to test separately the thinking abilities of the two surgically separated halves of the human brain. They found that *each half of the brain has its own separate train of conscious thought and its own memories.* Even more important, they found that *the two sides of the brain think in fundamentally different ways*: While the left brain tends to think in words, the right brain thinks directly in sensory images.

The two halves of the brain thus have a kind of partnership in which the left brain handles language and logical thinking, while the right does things that are difficult to put into words. By thinking in images instead of words, the right brain can recognize a face in a crowd or put together

---

* For simplicity we will temporarily ignore the fact that about 5 per cent of the population (one third of all left-handed people) have speech in the right brain and nonverbal thinking in the left. This is discussed further in Chapter 7.

the pieces of a jigsaw puzzle, which would totally baffle the left brain.

A Left-Right Division of Labor

In all mammals there is a natural left-right division of labor which is inherent in their neural "wiring": Each half of the brain is connected only to the *opposite* side of the body.[1] Vision, sense of touch, and movement on the right is thus the job of the left brain and vice versa. The nerve connections between the hemispheres (see Figure 1) make it possible for each to exchange information so that either hemisphere can directly or indirectly enable one to see, feel, or move on either side of the body.†

Split-brain patients, however, have had an operation in which these nerve connections are cut (to prevent the spread of epileptic seizures). As a result *the hemispheres of their brain are totally isolated from each other, and each hemisphere can see, feel, and move only the opposite side of their body.* Though the split-brain patient still appears quite normal to the casual observer, closer examination shows that he acts very much like two separate people in one body. The "person" that we can talk to (his left brain) sees and feels only on his right side. His left hand and left field of vision are controlled by a separate mind (his right

† For example, the left hemisphere has direct neural connections to the right side of the body. It can also move the left side of the body indirectly by sending movement commands across the corpus callosum to the right hemisphere. Left-side vision and touch information is also available because the right hemisphere sends it across via the corpus callosum. (See Appendix II for a summary of left-right nerve connections.)

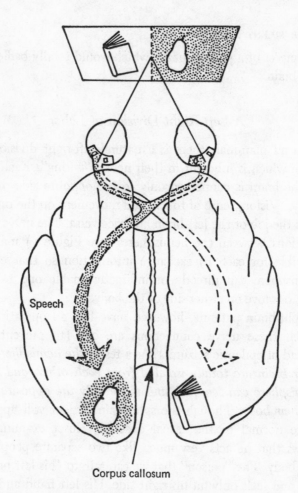

2. *Optic nerve connections in a normal person connect only half of the visual field to each hemisphere. If a person fixes his eyes on a point, the right hemisphere will see only things to the left while the left hemisphere will see things to the right. Normally the left and right hemispheres inform each other of what they see via the corpus callosum; but in split-brain patients, separation of vision is complete.*

brain), which cannot speak to us but can independently learn, solve complex problems, and even react with emotion.

This separate right-brain consciousness is obvious when a split-brain patient touches a hidden object with his left hand. If we ask him what he is handling, he will insist he does not know—yet his left hand can easily point it out among a collection of other objects. If asked how he knew which object to point to, he will answer something like "I guessed" or "I did it unconsciously."

Since each hand of the split-brain patient is controlled by a different hemisphere, it is possible to study each side of the brain as one would study two different people. For example, the block design test is a common test for nonverbal intelligence which requires assembling colored blocks to form specified patterns. The split-brain patient finds this test almost impossible with his right hand, yet he scores normally with his left. Yet with a verbal task such as writing a sentence, the left hand becomes the inept one: Writing is normal with the right hand, but impossible with the left.

Two Kinds of Thinking

After hundreds of experiments, a clear pattern of the abilities of the two hemispheres finally emerged, proving that the two halves of our brain think in distinctly different ways. As the language specialist, the left brain not only thinks in words; it excels at the kind of one-step-at-a-time logical sequences that are the basis of language. Because the right brain thinks in images, it has a tremendous advantage for recognizing and manipulating complex visual patterns.

When a normal person does a nonverbal task like the block design test, he clearly does it with his right brain. When he does a verbal task such as writing a sentence, control comes from the left brain. This has been confirmed by measuring electrical activity (EEG) in each half of the brain while people do various tasks. During a block design test the right brain is more active (less alpha); writing sentences makes the left brain more active.[2]

Words and logic are powerful tools for thinking, and the left brain easily outperforms the right in tasks where they are useful. But the right brain comes into its own in matters that are difficult to put into words or understand in logical steps—the things that you must "have a feel for." Try, for example, to describe *verbally* the configuration of lines used to represent a cube on a piece of paper (see Figure 3). The impossibility of verbalizing such concepts is dramatically demonstrated by the split-brain patient's futile attempts at drawing with his right hand (left brain).

Another specialty of the right brain is recognition of disguised or fragmented shapes. If fragments of a shape are felt with the left hand, the split-brain patient has no difficulty associating the fragments with the complete shape. However, if the other hand is used, only the most obvious associations can be made.‡ Since this ability to recognize things in altered form is a crucial part of creativity, the right brain takes on new importance.

‡ These and other experiments are covered in detail in Chapters 9 to 11.

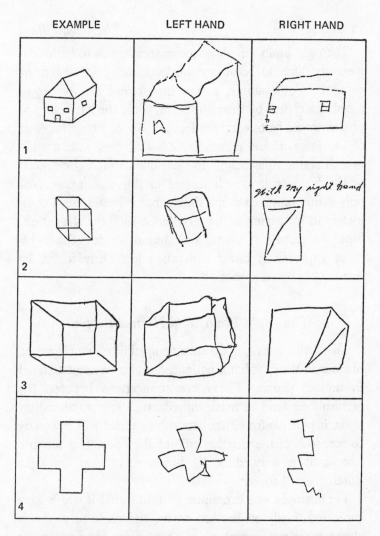

EXAMPLE	LEFT HAND	RIGHT HAND

With my right hand

3. Spatial concepts and drawing are done better by the right hemisphere. Though right-hand muscle control is better, the incorrect relationships between the features show the left brain's ineptness with spatial concepts.

The right brain's mode of recognition seems to be fundamentally different because it works on an entire image "in parallel." For example, a face in a crowd can be recognized at a glance by the right brain, while the left-brain approach would be to compare features one at a time for each of the faces. If the person is "tall and dark with a wide mouth and a moustache," the left brain would check each of the faces against each feature in this description. Not only is this approach much slower, but it breaks down completely if, for example, the moustache has been shaved off. Since "a picture is worth a thousand words," the right-brain approach is faster and much less easily fooled by missing or altered details.

The "Split Brain" and Normal People

All of the left-right differences in ability, which are so obvious in the split-brain patient, can also be demonstrated in normal people. The nerve connections between the hemispheres tend to mask the effects, however, since they make it possible for either hemisphere directly or indirectly to see, feel, or move either side of the body. If a recognition task is very difficult, however, a clear left-right difference will appear.

For example, one experimenter found that if words were projected briefly on the left or the right side of a screen, they were correctly recognized about twice as often on the right (by the word-oriented left brain). Faces produced the opposite result, with almost twice as many correct identifications when they were flashed on the left. This effect has been used for decades by military aircraft spotters, who are trained to look just to the right of the aircraft so it will be in the left half of their visual field.

Another method of demonstrating the left-right differences in normal people is the dichotic listening test. When different words are heard simultaneously by each ear, a person will tend to report the words heard on the right and ignore those heard on the left. If the same test is done using music or natural sounds, the advantage reverses to the left ear. Again, the right brain is better at recognition of things that are not easily put into words.

The most amazing thing about split-brain patients is that, in spite of the fact that they have two separate minds, they generally feel and act like normal people. The split-brain operation was performed on at least twenty-five people before 1944, yet the published summaries of all twenty-five case histories specifically state that no change in the patients' mental abilities was observed.[8]

Two of these patients were reexamined some years later[4] and found to have the same separation of left and right consciousness found in the newer patients. Though they really have two separate minds in one body, their doctors had failed to notice it! Dramatic as these effects are under special lab conditions, they can go completely unnoticed in the routine situations of normal life.

If the effects of a split-brain operation are subtle enough to go unnoticed, perhaps the normal mind is not as singular as we once thought. After all, split-brain patients notice no difference in their own consciousness after their operation. They are able to return to public schools or family life, and one patient was even found to have a full-scale IQ of 103 after his operation.[5]

This ability to feel and act normally even though the two halves of the brain are split strongly suggests that much of a normal person's behavior is really just the result of his left or right brain acting independently. The subtle deficits of the split-brain patient are confined to the areas of behavior that require information to be passed between the halves of the brain. Otherwise, these patients act "normally" under the control of one hemisphere or the other. When they say they notice no change in their consciousness, their left brain is in control. When they are being tested for left-handed block assembly or shape recognition, their right brain takes control and they pass into a clearly nonverbal state.

When we ask a split-brain patient to explain actions that *we* know were done by their right brain, they sometimes verbally explain their actions with rationalizations that we know are untrue—but they obviously don't. Evidently, their left-brain consciousness has constructed a false world in which it is responsible for all actions. When it observes a left-handed response that *we* know came from the right brain, it will often make up a story to explain the response.

For example, in one experiment different pictures were flashed simultaneously on the left and the right of a screen, and the subject had to choose simultaneously a matching picture with each hand. In one case[6] a snow scene was flashed on the left while a chicken claw was flashed on the right. As expected, the subject's left hand chose a snow shovel while his right hand chose a chicken. When asked why his left hand had picked a shovel, he answered, "I see a claw and I picked a chicken, and you have to clean out the chicken shed with a shovel." Since the split-brain patient's left brain doesn't hesitate to rationalize and take credit for actions that are obviously the work of his right brain, one can't help wondering how often normal people do the same thing.

A Working Relationship

Occasionally the split-brain patient has a problem when *both* hemispheres try to take control. A film of the first split-brain patient shows his left hand impatiently trying to help his right hand do a block arrangement test. After being stopped twice by the experimenter, he finally sits on his left hand to keep it still. After continued frustration with the right hand, the experimenter tells him to try both hands. A battle ensues in which the two hands fight for control, with one tearing down the work of the other.

Conflicts of this type are relatively rare because the two hemispheres develop a working relationship. Each hemisphere is capable of inhibiting the other if it "feels more strongly" that it can solve the problem. In tasks that require quick response, control normally passes to the hemisphere that is first to have an answer. Experimenters have shown that they can increase a hemisphere's chances of taking control by intentionally giving it encouragement. For example, after the right brain has successfully solved a long sequence of problems, it will often try to perform a task that would normally have been done by the left hemisphere.

The working relationship between the left and right brains is developed much the same as any partnership develops. A slight advantage for one hemisphere is magnified with time as its partner increasingly stands back to let it handle a particular task. Ideally, each hemisphere does what it is best equipped to do, but bad habits can easily develop in which the wrong hemisphere prevails and prevents true abilities from being expressed.

The single-mind concept is essentially a left-brain verbal concept that ignores the contribution of the right brain. Unfortunately, educational theory is so dominated by this concept that left-brain approaches are often encouraged when they are not really appropriate. Any partnership in which one partner is both silent and invisible is bound to develop in a lopsided way.

Even the basic left-right specialization of verbal and nonverbal thinking is developed gradually as a result of the left-right competitive process. Up to the age of about five, either hemisphere is able to develop full language capability. However, since the left brain has a *slight* inborn tendency to respond to speech sounds, it wins the competition for speech control. As the years go by, this advantage steadily increases. Since language requires a step-by-step rather than holistic approach, the right brain is more and more able to dominate in nonverbal, spatial, and visual thinking.

The basis of much brain surgery is that damaged brain tissue can win the left-right competition and prevent healthy tissue from doing the job. For example, if a child's left brain is damaged, it will continue to control speech in a faulty way and prevent development of speech in the right brain. *If the entire left hemisphere is removed before the age of five, normal speech will develop in the right hemisphere.*

If, however, the left hemisphere is removed or damaged *after* speech has fully developed, there is no hope of establishing anything but the crudest language ability. The basic organization used for nonverbal thinking is so different from the one used for language and verbal thinking that no amount of retraining can change it.

Surgical Removal of One Hemisphere

When a hemisphere is surgically removed (hemispherectomy) in an adult, the change in the patient is a dramatic demonstration of the contribution of each hemisphere. Removal of the right hemisphere (left brain intact) leaves language basically unimpaired but somewhat computerlike. While the precise *literal* meaning of words is understood perfectly, metaphor, inflection, and emotional tone are not. Personality, insight, imagination, and initiative also suffer greatly. Simple spatial tasks such as putting a shirt on right side up or finding the way back from the bathroom become very confusing.

In spite of the severe handicaps following loss of the right brain, the patient often continues to insist that everything is normal. After a lifetime of rationalizing the right brain's contributions as its own, the left brain now goes to extreme lengths to keep together the single-mind model.

When asked about certain obvious handicaps, the patient will often construct far-fetched excuses. For example, since he can no longer move his left hand,* he may claim that it is not his hand at all.

Perhaps the clearest demonstration that the verbal consciousness is unaware of the right brain's thoughts is the fact that *the entire right hemisphere can be removed from a conscious person without his noticing any difference!* One surgeon reported that in four right hemispherectomies "conversation with the patients was carried on throughout the operation without any significant change in conscious state."[7] (Since the brain feels no pain, brain surgery is often done with the patient conscious.)

Many split-brain operations were also done with the patient conscious. Again, running conversations were held with the patients to monitor their mental functions.[8] Since the patient's verbal consciousness noticed no change, it is clear that it was not aware of the right brain's thoughts.

Since our verbal concept of consciousness is confined to the left hemisphere, we might expect removal of that hemisphere to eliminate consciousness. Several cases have been reported in which mature patients have had their entire *left* hemisphere removed to stop a spreading tumor. Though they lost their ability to *talk* about consciousness (or anything else), they definitely remained conscious, thinking people. In fact, their emotional tone and nonverbal personality remained essentially intact. One forty-

* Remember that each hemisphere has nerve connections only to the *opposite* hand and foot. Normally the left brain moves the left hand by sending a motion command over the corpus callosum to the right brain, which actually does the moving on an automatic level.

seven-year-old patient† had a performance (nonverbal) IQ of 110 five months after his left brain was removed. This places him in the top 25 per cent of the population in nonverbal intelligence!

Clearly the right brain, which has a consciousness of its own, is an important part of a whole person; yet it is ignored by the verbal consciousness of the left brain. Just as we have learned through indirect evidence to think of the earth as a sphere, we can learn to be aware of both sides of our own mind. The nonverbal consciousness that the left hemispherectomy patient feels so strongly is present in all of us, if we will just learn to recognize it. First we must overcome a lifetime habit of acknowledging only thoughts that can be expressed in words.

† More about this and other hemispherectomy cases in Chapter 10.

Chapter 2

THE "UNCONSCIOUS MIND"— DISCOVERED

Imagine two schoolboys who have ditched their algebra class. Both boys hate algebra and find it impossible to understand. They much prefer playing softball, and delightedly throw the ball to each other as far as they can. Each time the ball is thrown, the boy catching it effortlessly estimates its speed and trajectory, compensates for wind and the slope of the ground, and catches the ball beautifully. In doing so, they are showing a very sophisticated nonverbal understanding of physics which they could not begin to explain. This is real knowledge based on nonverbal learning. And from this knowledge, they are able to solve problems far more complex than the equations in the algebra class they are avoiding. In fact, even if they complete college and receive a degree in physics, they would probably never be able to write equations that would predict where the ball will land as well as they now do automatically.

This imaginary scene illustrates the contrast between the right-brain method of handling a problem and the verbal, left-brain approach. Both approaches require the development of a separate fund of knowledge. It is possible to be an expert at one and have no knowledge of the other. The opposite situation might be a Ph.D. in math who programs gunnery computers to solve projectile problems, yet can't throw a ball as well as a schoolboy. While it is possible to have both a verbal and a nonverbal understanding of the problem, one does not follow from the other. This is really the same as saying that the left and the right brain have *separate but overlapping stores of knowledge*.

Since the left and right brains are organized differently, it is easy to see why the memories of one are not useful to the other. The right brain looks at the *entire* situation all at once and reacts according to what it has learned. The mathematical equations in the memory of the left brain are obviously not useful with this approach. The left brain, on the other hand, handles complexity by sequences of small logical steps. The right brain's holistic "feel" for throwing a ball on a windy hill is likewise of no use to the left brain. The two kinds of brain organization simply store knowledge in a different form—almost like a different language.

If we were to ask the two schoolboys how they throw the ball, most likely we would find that *verbally they don't know* how they do it. If you press them for an explanation, they would try to give you one. But they would probably have to throw the ball and *watch themselves* to figure it out. You could just as well ask another person to watch them and verbalize how it is done. In a sense it *is* another person because their left-brain consciousness *hasn't really been paying attention* while the right brain learned to throw and catch. The left consciousness thus must actually *watch* the right brain's actions and try to verbalize how it is done by deduction.

If we look at an intellectually inclined adult who has taken lots of lessons in a sport, we may find an opposite pattern. He may *play* poorly, yet *talk* endlessly about theory and proper form. In this case a habitual tendency to use the left brain has reversed the situation: The right brain learns little, as it is constantly pushed aside by the left brain's attempts to "keep the knee bent" or "put the weight on the left heel."

One of the most dramatic demonstrations of our dual consciousness is the actual battle that many people fight with themselves when they play tennis or golf. After a bad shot, many players get angry and berate themselves verbally. We know that the left brain does the talking—but to whom is it talking?

Since the left-brain approach is too slow and systematic to use during an actual shot, the verbal consciousness yields control and then takes over again with a comment like "Damn it! Keep the elbow bent." The relationship between the left and right consciousnesses is almost like that between a verbal coach and a silent player. In some people it is easy to see the verbal coach's bad temper and impatience upsetting the silent player's performance. One can't help being reminded of the incident in which the split-brain patient's left and right hands fought over "who" would do a block assembly test.

One of the first real effects of the right-brain revolution

is an understanding of this process in sports. Tim Gallwey developed the idea of cooperation between the two consciousnesses in his best-selling book *The Inner Game of Tennis*. Another book, *Inner Skiing*, is now revolutionizing the teaching of skiing.

A new understanding of these two modes of thought can dramatically increase our abilities by helping us to fit the approach to the task. Many highly educated, intellectual people habitually try to use their left brain for totally inappropriate tasks. Their right brain can virtually atrophy, making them totally inept, not just in sports, art, and dancing, but with the truly *creative* side of intellectual pursuits.

The classic left-brain approach to dancing is a perfect example of doing something the hard way with appalling results. By emphasizing the learning of "steps" as a discrete sequence of foot movements, the simple and natural act of moving the body to music can be turned into an intellectual exercise. The ideal learning aid for this approach is a piece of paper marked with numbered footprints, which you put on the floor and follow by stepping on the numbers in order. After much effort and practice, the result usually looks so bad that most engineers, lawyers, and other left-brain types pretend that they never tried to learn.

If you ask any really good dancer how to do a dance, he will naturally reply, "Like this," and proceed to show you. If you press him for a verbal explanation, he will probably have to do the step and *watch himself* before he can explain. This is another case of nonverbal knowledge to which the left-brain consciousness has no access. The dancer's verbal explanation will be no better than what a mere observer could deduce from watching the right brain's demonstration of the step. A professional dance teacher, of course, will learn the steps both verbally and nonverbally. The verbal descriptions may satisfy your left brain's desire to "learn" how to dance; but they will be very little help in getting the real *feel* of dancing. To really learn to dance, your right brain must take control and learn by watching and imitating.

Music is another area where a right- or a left-brain approach can be used. Just as it is possible for a machine to play piano (a player piano), it is possible to learn left-brain piano playing. Each note simply represents a key, and with long practice one can learn to sight-read music properly. Playing by ear seems to be a completely different ability, which has little relation to reading music. While it is possible to develop both abilities, knowing one is little help in learning the other. Again, it appears that the left and right brains develop separate knowledge, each encoded in a different way. One interesting confirmation of this interpretation is the case of an amateur musician who suffered a right-brain tumor.[1] He remained able to sight-read music, but lost the ability to sing and play the piano from memory.

Intuition

While right-brain knowledge is useful in many physical activities, it is also crucial in a variety of purely mental activities. *Intuition* is a catch-all word for thinking processes that we can't *verbally* explain. Yet if we look at the characteristics of intuition, it is obvious that we are referring to right-brain functions: Intuitive judgments are not arrived at step by step, but in an instant. They typically take into consideration a large mass of data *in parallel*, without separately considering each factor. Finally, they cannot be explained verbally.

If we take the plans for a house we want built to an experienced contractor, he may glance over them for about ten minutes and tell us what it will cost and how long it will take. This is an *intuitive* judgment. Another approach he could use would be to add up every item on the bill of materials, calculate the price, one item at a time, then schedule each stage of the construction and estimate building time. With experience, the intuitive judgment can be as accurate as the methodical one. If you ask him to explain the intuitive estimate, he might say something like "gut feel" or "experience." In actual fact, the intuitive approach is a result of right-brain thinking: Just as it can recognize a face in a crowd at one glance, the right brain can analyze large masses of data and make a judgment in one step.

As with any ability, intuitive judgment can be developed or allowed to atrophy, depending on how much it is used and how much confidence we have in its results. There are, of course, situations where it would be foolish to use intuition. For instance, glancing at a complex math problem and "estimating" the answer by intuition will obviously not work. There is most definitely a place for intuition even in a left-brain science such as mathematics. Most creative breakthroughs, even in math, are a result of an "intuitive leap" that must then be carefully analyzed in logical terms by looking at the result, almost as an outsider would.

Though intuition has been used since before recorded

history, it has always had a sort of "black magic" quality about it. Now that we understand its physical basis, we can begin to develop it more intelligently.

The Right Brain as "Unconscious Mind"

Since the right brain has always been with us, the products of its thinking have been impossible to ignore. Intuition is one of many abstract concepts created to name these phenomena.

Freud originated the concepts of "conscious" and "unconscious" mental processes to help explain human behavior. The characteristics of these concepts are strikingly similar to what we know about the right and left brains respectively. Perhaps our knowledge of the right brain can also raise these concepts out of the world of the theoretical and into the world of physical proof.

What makes the unconscious mind unconscious is the fact that, though it influences our behavior, we have difficulty in *verbally* explaining its actions. We have already discussed examples of right-brain knowledge that cannot be verbalized by the left-brain consciousness. While our right brain is also a part of our consciousness, its thoughts are necessarily separate from those of the verbal left brain. Since each hemisphere is organized differently and stores memories in a different "language," it would be chaotic if the thoughts of the two "mixed" freely. Nature's solution is to keep them separate except for certain limited interactions which are so subtle that they are hardly missed when they are cut in the split-brain patient.

Many of the psychiatric techniques for probing the "unconscious mind" make use of the right brain's superiority at certain tasks. In the Rorschach test, one interprets an "ink blot" as a picture, making use of the right brain's superiority at recognizing fragmented or incomplete information. Similarly, in free association a single word acts as a stimulus for the right brain to make an association (probably by retrieving an image). The left brain, which makes more literal associations, is at a disadvantage without a complete phrase.

Because the two halves of the brain essentially think in different languages, the memories of one hemisphere are not directly available to the other. This has recently been proven experimentally:[2] During a test in which only their left hemisphere was anesthetized,* patients were given a hidden object to feel with their left hand. After the drug effects wore off and the patients' speech returned, they were asked to name the object they felt. Even after considerable probing, the patients were unable to do so. When the object was displayed visually along with several other items, the patients recognized it immediately! Apparently *the nonverbal memory of the object stored by the right brain was not available to the verbal consciousness of the left hemisphere.* However, as soon as the object was seen, the right hemisphere recognized it.

The psychiatric implications of this finding are far-

* This test is called the Wada procedure. Since each hemisphere is fed by a different artery in the neck, they can be individually anesthetized by injecting a sedative in one side or the other. By observing which side causes loss of speech, the hemisphere controlling speech can be positively determined.

reaching: A memory can actually exist which affects behavior, yet it is unknown and unavailable to the verbal consciousness! Much psychiatric treatment seems to be directed at bringing out the nonverbal memories and making the verbal consciousness aware of them. While this may help make our words more consistent with our deeds, it does not change the "gut feel" responses of the right brain.

Two Minds—Two Personalities

One of the things that help unify the left and right brains is the fact that they inhabit the same body and see the world through the same pair of eyes. However, since each of these two minds has its own orientation, they experience things differently.

Take, for instance, a conversation with another person. The left brain generally responds to the literal meaning of the words it hears and will not even notice the meaning of inflection. The right brain perceives different aspects of the same conversation: Tone of voice, facial expression, and body language are noticed while the words are relatively less important.

This is a two-way process. The words are *coming from* the other person's left brain, and the tone of voice, facial expression, and body language are coming from his right brain. Thus, the conversation is going on simultaneously on two levels. In fact, when two people interact, they actually form two separate relationships:

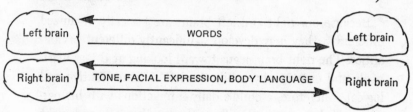

The memories and impressions formed by the left and right consciousnesses may be completely different.

The right-brain impression is what we would call an "unconscious" one. We would feel it as a "gut level" response, but would probably not be able to verbalize it. Since our right brain is capable of controlling our behavior, we may well act in a way that conflicts with our verbal consciousness' conception of how we should act. It was this kind of behavior that made the original concept of the "unconscious mind" necessary.

Since much of our emotional behavior is under the control of the right brain, a person can have a different set of childhood memories in his right brain than in his left.[3] Consider, for example, a punishment in which the parent says, "I'm doing this because I love you," but has a facial expression and tone of voice that says, "I hate you." The right- and left-brain memories of the incident would be quite different. The right brain could initiate behavior based on its interpretation of the memory, which would conflict with the left brain's retelling of the incident to the psychiatrist. It may look like a case of "repression" because the verbal description of the memory doesn't agree with the patient's behavior.

Because our right and left brains are basically organized differently, they may develop significantly different personalities. The right brain leans toward looking at things negatively and emotionally, while the left is more positive and logical. Therefore, a child's daily interactions with his parents will be perceived differently by the left and right brains. If the parents present opposing messages from their left and right brains, the "upbringing" of the two hemispheres of a child may differ significantly. Fluctuations of mood and behavior may be partly a result of variations in the relative activity of these two separate personalities.

It is even possible to observe separately fluctuating moods in the left and right brains. Our performance in sports is very dependent on mood and attention; but the fluctuations in right-brain mood as indicated by physical performance do not necessarily coincide with the mood we feel in our verbal left brain. Sexual performance likewise has fluctuations based on right-brain mood, which do not necessarily coincide with the mood we feel in our left brain. It is almost as though two different people are involved: one who *talks* about sex and the other who *does* it.

An experiment at the University of Oklahoma[4] showed that drinking alcohol dulls the right brain more than the left. It was found that response time in a shape-finding task slowed by 37 per cent in the left half of the visual field versus only 6 per cent on the right. If the right brain gets drunk before the left brain, this could explain why drunks are often "all talk and no action" when it comes to sex. Experiments at UCLA[5] show that marijuana has the opposite effect: EEG testing shows a change in the alpha ratio indicating an increase in right-brain activity relative to left. Talk in general is thus reduced while sexual "action" may increase.

Dreams and the Right Brain

Freud called dreams "the royal road to the unconscious." There is evidence that dreaming occurs primarily in the right brain. Certainly the content of many dreams has the characteristics of right-brain activity: Dreams are often *nonverbal, emotional,* full of *images,* and lacking in a logical time sequence.

In some cases brain damage to the right brain will cause patients who previously dreamed vividly to stop dreaming entirely.[6] In addition to losing the ability to dream, these patients also lose the ability to form visual images in their mind when they are awake.

Further evidence that dreams originate in the right brain was found by brain surgeon Wilder Penfield.[7] Before surgery on epileptics, Penfield would apply small electrical currents to various points on the surface of the brain to locate the area of the brain responsible for the seizures. A local anesthetic was used on the scalp so the patient could be awake during the entire procedure. Stimulation on the *right* side of the brain would often induce "dreamlike states" in which the patients experienced flashbacks of memories or visual illusions. Here are some examples of the patients' actual words in describing their hallucinations:

"Dream is starting—there are a lot of people in the living room—one of them is my mother."

"Yes, Doctor! Yes, Doctor! Now I hear people laughing —my friends—in South Africa."

"A familiar sight danced into my mind and away again."

"Yes. I heard voices down along the river somewhere— a man's voice and a woman's voice calling—I think I saw the river."

The fascinating thing about these illusions is that the patients experience a sort of *double consciousness*. They are aware that they are in the operating room talking to the doctor, and, at the same time, they feel that they are *actually experiencing* the hallucination. These experiences resulted only from stimulation of the *right* side of the brain. Stimulation of the *left* side affected various speech or muscle movements, but never caused hallucinations or double consciousness. Since a normal person never experiences this double consciousness, it appears that the electrical stimulation defeated the normal system, which activates either the right *or* the left brain's consciousness: Though the left-brain consciousness is activated, the stimulation causes some right-brain memory traces to be triggered, which gives a feeling of dual consciousness. In schizophrenia, the mechanism that activates only the left *or* right apparently breaks down, causing a spillover of dreamlike[8] images into the normal waking consciousness.

Verbally recalling dreams that originate in the right brain requires a transferal of images from the right to the left brain. Several of the split-brain patients who had vivid dreams before their operation reported that they didn't dream at all after their operation.[9] Their dreams may still be occurring in their right hemisphere, but their left brain is now unaware of them because of the cut neural connections.

Most people who say that they don't dream are probably not transferring the right-brain images to their verbal consciousness. Sleep researchers have found that everyone has several periods each night of rapid eye movement (REM) which correspond to dreaming. If a subject is awakened during a REM period, he will invariably say that he was dreaming and can usually describe the dream. In one experiment at the University of Edinburgh,[10] the subjects were classified before testing as to "cognitive style." One group was scientifically oriented, logical, *convergent* thinking types, while the other group was classified as *divergent* —less logical and more artistic. The subjects were awakened each time their eye movements indicated they were dreaming and were asked to describe their dreams. The convergent (left brain) types could only describe their dreams 65 per cent of the time while the divergent types recalled 95.2 per cent of their dreams. Many logical, convergent thinkers may have such a strong habit of using their left brain and ignoring their right that they have lost touch with the dream activity of the right brain.

As the night progresses, dreams have more and more left-brain characteristics.[11] For example, verbal activity is reported in only 30 per cent of dreams early in the night. However, the percentage gradually rises to almost 100 per cent just before waking. The ability to recall the dream likewise rises gradually from 20 per cent early in the night

to 80 per cent before waking. This is confirmed by EEG
readings, which indicate more right-hemisphere activity
during early evening dreaming.[12] As the night progresses,
this differential gradually decreases. After allowing the
right brain to have free rein much of the night, the left
brain may gradually reestablish its hold on the consciousness in preparation for waking.

Psychiatrists have found that dreams are an excellent
way to discover the "repressed" thoughts of the "unconscious" mind. With practice, people can learn to pay more
attention to their dreams and improve their dream recall.
Practice at dream recall may thus be a good way to improve the flow of information between the right and left
brains.

Is the Unconscious Mind Really Conscious?

The concept of an unconscious mind was created to explain the obvious gap between our behavior and the
thoughts we observe in our mind by introspection. When
we look into our mind and describe, analyze, or discuss
what we see, we do so with *words*. Therefore, nonverbal
thoughts and memories of the right brain are ignored. In
an attempt to rationalize the obvious gap, the left brain
attributes the results of the right brain's thoughts to some
mysterious entity called the "unconscious mind."

These thoughts are conscious in their own way, but not
in the way the left brain recognizes. If we "unconsciously"
fear somebody, we actually *feel* as well as act on that fear.
That we cannot *explain* the fear or describe reasons in our

verbal memory for it causes us (and psychiatrists) to call it "unconscious." When we are absorbed in right-brain physical activity or intuitive thought, we don't feel unconscious. We can even *feel* the thought process; but we *can't describe it in words.*

The word "consciousness" actually has two separate meanings depending on the context. *Objective consciousness* can be judged by an outsider, as it is based on external observations of such things as reflexes, reactions, and intelligence. *Subjective consciousness*, however, is being conscious of our own consciousness. It is something that we feel inside ourselves and is very much influenced by our own philosophical interpretations. Introspection is completely subjective and, thus, easily distorted by our own preconceived expectations and imagination. It is not surprising, then, that we can completely ignore the "feelings" of nonverbal consciousness.

The adult left-hemispherectomy (intact right brain) cases mentioned in Chapter 1 are clearly conscious in the *objective* sense. Though unable to speak, they have normal reactions consistent with their personality and can even do well on nonverbal IQ tests. Though they cannot discuss it with you, it is obvious that they also consider themselves *subjectively conscious.* The consciousness they feel is the very one that we deny exists when we talk about the "unconscious mind." While we can fool ourselves with words into ignoring the nonverbal consciousness, these patients feel conscious yet have *only* nonverbal consciousness.

With a little practice, we can expand our introspection beyond the strictly verbal and "feel" the effects of both kinds of consciousness. For example, when we are totally absorbed in a nonverbal activity such as skiing, jogging, drawing, dancing, or making love, our verbal consciousness should essentially be "switched off." If we later try to use our verbal consciousness to remember how we felt during that time, we find that there is a sort of gap in our memory. General, snapshotlike impressions may come to mind; but the linear time record in our verbal memory has a definite gap. Though it is hard to *describe* the feeling of right-brain consciousness, it is definitely not "unconsciousness."

Actually, both our objective and subjective consciousnesses are the sum total of thoughts, knowledge, and feelings of both the left and the right brains. If one hemisphere is removed from an adult's brain, certain aspects of that consciousness will be lost in the subjective and the objective senses. Either hemisphere alone can think, feel, and remember in its own way. However, only the left hemisphere can *express* its awareness of its own thoughts in words. Because of the right brain's inability to express itself, it has been unfairly called "the unconscious mind." A better choice of words might be "the nonverbal mind."

Chapter 3

CREATIVITY AND
THE RIGHT BRAIN

It has long been known by creative people that the "unconscious mind" has a crucial role in all creative thought. While creativity in art, music, and dance can often function with very little help from verbal left-brain processes, most creative work requires a healthy cooperation between intuition and logical thought. In most intellectual fields, for example, the real creative breakthroughs are the result of intuition. Intuition itself, however, is generally useless until it can be verified and described verbally and logically.

Logic and language are at the basis of most modern progress because they make it possible for one person to communicate his insights to another. Knowledge is thus built upon knowledge, from the successive thinking of many people. With logic, one can prove the truth of an insight so that others may act upon it. But logic and language are so rigidly structured that they are not suitable for the kind of flexible thinking that *finds* creative breakthroughs. When we think verbally, we are limited by the constraints of our verbal memory.

Verbal meaning is largely determined by the *order* in which words occur. For example, "Tom hits Bill" has a different meaning from "Bill hits Tom." In order to preserve meaning, our verbal memory must then preserve the order of sequences of words. The visual memory system of our right brain has no such limitation: We can remember a picture of Tom hitting Bill left to right, right to left, top to bottom, etc., without losing the meaning. This additional flexibility turns out to be crucial in creative thinking. It means that both thoughts and memories don't have to be "taken literally."

We can see the inflexibility of our verbal memory immediately if we simply try to spell a long word backward. Though we can recite the letters quickly in the "normal" order, the letters just can't be retrieved in reverse order. The same thing is true of a well-learned sentence (for example, try saying the first line of the Lord's Prayer backward). Probably the easiest way to spell a word backward is to form a mental image of the word and read off the letters from right to left. This is "cheating," of course, because you are then using your visual memory.

If somebody asks you to describe the contents of your living room, you can call up a mental image which makes everything in your visual span available to you at once. To describe the image, you must convert it into a serial stream of words; you would typically answer by going around the room clockwise and listing the contents one item at a time.

You could just as well give a description by going around the room counterclockwise or even randomly. Your visual memory is so flexible that it is not limited to a particular time sequence.

Thinking is very much dependent on memory because when we think, we are really just combining and rearranging the contents of our memory. Mental abilities are thus determined by the characteristics of memory, just as the speed and power of a computer are limited by its memory's size and speed. The memory in a computer is very much like our own verbal memory because everything must be done in a sequence—one step at a time. The problem with this approach is that if one piece of data is missing or in the wrong form, no solution is possible. This is the reason why left-brain thinking and computers both have great power, yet practically no creativity.

To build a creative computer, we would need a memory element like the visual memory of the right brain. But scientists haven't the least notion of how to build such a memory—much less a complete computer. To understand what this means, look at the excerpt below from a test on visual intelligence. An average person can look at each drawing of a hand and decide whether it is a left or right hand in only a couple of seconds, yet the largest supercomputer known would be incapable of doing this task at all.

Though we can easily solve the hand problem with visual thinking and even answer verbally "left" or "right," our left brain is simply receiving the answer from the right brain. This becomes apparent if we try to explain verbally

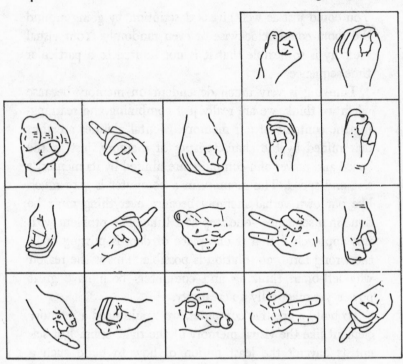

5. *Thurstone's Hand Test. Which of these hands are left hands and which are right?*

how we got the answer. The fact is that *we don't know* verbally how we got the answer because the task is impossible to do verbally. If we try to watch our own mind when we solve the problem, we will find nothing more than a vague "feeling" or "visualization" of imaginary hands, which is our right brain at work. The kind of verbal thoughts that some people who talk to themselves actually articulate are completely absent.* The best explanation for how we got our answer would be "by intuition."

Some Experiments with Visual Memory

Since visual memory deals with an entire image as a single unit, the actual amount of information that it can hold is staggering. Ralph Haber, of the University of Rochester,[2] showed subjects 2,560 photographic slides each at a rate of one slide every ten seconds. Two of the subjects saw 1,280 pictures a day during four-hour sessions on two consecutive days. The rest of the subjects saw only 640 slides a day on four consecutive days.

One hour after the end of the last viewing session, each subject was shown 280 pairs of slides—side by side on the same screen. One of the slides in each pair had been seen before and the other had not. When the subjects were asked which slide they had seen before, 85 to 95 per cent of their choices were correct! The two subjects who saw 1,280 slides a day did just as well as the subjects with a more leisurely viewing schedule. One can't help wondering what are the limits of the visual memory.

Actually, these results are not surprising when you relate

* Almost half of the population may actually make slight movements of their vocal apparatus during verbal thinking. When breathing rhythms were recorded during verbal thought, one experimenter[1] found that thirty of sixty-seven subjects had an irregular rhythm superimposed on their normal breathing. This irregular rhythm disappeared when the subjects were solving a problem designed to require visual thinking. Pure spatial problems like the hands test cause the talk to be replaced by a "feeling" or images.

them to what happens when you take a vacation. After weeks of traveling, each one of your vacation slides is familiar when you look at them later. Even postcards and related travelogue pictures are familiar years later. These, of course, are selected scenes from tens of thousands you may have observed and remembered on the vacation.

What's astonishing is that visual memory is capable of remembering orientation, but has no problem ignoring it. Eight of the subjects in Haber's slide viewing experiment were shown their slides *reversed* so that a tree on the left became a tree on the right. Again, the scores were virtually unaffected. Four of the subjects were asked to tell whether or not the slides were reversed and were able to respond correctly in most instances. This ability to recognize without being fooled by unimportant differences like orientation, lighting, and distance was extremely important in the evolution of mankind. Visual memory was important to early humans for finding their way home from hunting or gathering food. Recognition was necessary even though the seasons or the time of day or the direction from which a scene was viewed changed.

This same ability to recognize things in an altered form or context is the basis of creative thinking. Creative breakthroughs generally are a result of finding hidden relationships—patterns that are obscured by their context. While this is the natural province of visual thinking, verbal thinking is inherently limited in its ability to make such abstract connections.

Visual and Verbal Thinking

One of the benefits of having two kinds of thinking is that they can often work together in a task. Lee Brooks, of McMaster University in Canada, demonstrated that visual and verbal thinking are separate processes. He did this by asking subjects to do visual or verbal mental tasks while reporting their answers either visually or verbally.

When the time required to do the tasks was compared, he found that performance was much better if the kind of thinking used in the task was not also needed for reporting the answers. For example, a visual task took more than twice as long if the answers were given visually rather than verbally. Yet a verbal task was 40 per cent faster when answers were given visually instead of verbally.[8]

Short-term memory, which is the basis of thought, exists as two separate processes—one verbal and the other visual. It is not possible to be thinking consciously in both hemispheres at once. For example, the verbal and the visual problem cannot be thought of at the same time. It is possible, however, for the thinking hemisphere to use the resources of the other hemisphere on an *automatic* level. When the right hemisphere is doing the visual thinking required by a visual problem, it is able to use the left hemisphere's speech capabilities to relay "yes" and "no" answers. This speech is on an automatic level and does not require the verbal consciousness to be activated.

Cognitive Style

The abilities and even the personality of an individual are strongly influenced by his "mental habits." One of the most important of these habits is a person's tendency to depend primarily on his left or right brain. Some tasks clearly demand left- or right-brain approaches. But the majority fall into a gray area where either the intuitive or the logical can be used with some success. People habitually favor one approach over the other.

Fortunately for some people, there are occupations in which one can function by relying on only one hemisphere all the time. Many athletes and artists, for example, are so nonverbal that they can hardly speak intelligibly. Rock, blues, and jazz musicians, for example, have a term called "soul," which represents the complete elimination of intellectualism in favor of feeling. Intellectual training does, in fact, tend to destroy the quality of "soul."

The polar opposite of the intuitive artist is the pure intellectual who verbalizes everything. Many of the "scholarly" fields such as literary criticism, education, and philosophy provide a refuge for left-brain types. While the real contributors to these fields combine insight and intuition with their verbal and logical abilities, a frighteningly large number of intellectuals have lost touch with reality. While words and logic are powerful tools, some people seem to forget that they are only meaningful as symbols of reality. Many "intellectual" discussions are no more than arguments about the meanings of words. The truly creative person uses logic and words as tools, yet knows their limitations.

How Creative People Think

Putting all theory aside, let us look at the real world of people who have proven to be truly creative. In 1945 a mathematician named Jacques Hadamard sent questionnaires to eminent mathematicians all over America asking them what kind of thinking they used in their creative work. He summarized the results as follows:[4]

> Practically all of them . . . avoid not only the use of mental words but also the mental use of algebraic or other precise signs. . . . The mental pictures of the mathematicians whose answers I have received are most frequently visual, but they may be of another kind—for instance, kinetic.

The real innovators in the precise and abstract science of mathematics rely heavily on visual thinking in their work. One particularly interesting reply came from one of the greatest thinkers of our time—Albert Einstein. Here are Einstein's own words:[5]

> (A) The words or the language, as they are written or spoken, do not seem to play any role in my mechanism of thought. The psychical entities which seem to serve as elements in thought are certain signs and more or less clear images which can be "voluntarily" reproduced and combined.
>
> There is, of course, a certain connection between those

elements and relevant logical concepts. It is also clear that
the desire to arrive finally at logically connected concepts
is the emotional basis of this rather vague play with the
above mentioned elements. But taken from a psychological
viewpoint, this combinatory play seems to be the essential
feature in productive thought—before there is any connection with logical construction in words or other kinds of
signs which can be communicated to others.

(B) The above mentioned elements are, in my case, of
visual and some of muscular type. Conventional words or
other signs have to be sought for laboriously only in a
secondary stage, when the mentioned associative play is
sufficiently established and can be reproduced at will.

Clearly, Einstein was in full touch with the consciousness of his right brain. The two stages of thinking he
described are obviously the mechanisms of the right and
left brains. The first stage uses the right brain's flexibility
and ability to hold and transform complex images in "visual" and "muscular" form. Only after a possible solution is
found in this way are words "laboriously" used to translate
the concept into a logical, verbal form. This pattern of
using each half of the brain for what it does best is seen
again and again in creative people.

Even Aristotle, the founder of formal logic, felt that imagery was necessary for thought. In *De Anima* (On the
Soul), he wrote:[6]

It is impossible even to think without a mental picture.
The same affection is involved in thinking as in drawing a
diagram.

Max Planck, the father of quantum theory, wrote in his autobiography that the creative scientist must have:[7]

> . . . a vivid intuitive imagination for new ideas not generated by deduction, but by *artistically* creative imagination.

Another organized inquiry into creative thinking was undertaken by American chemists Platt and Barker.[8] In this case, 83 per cent of the chemists who answered their questionnaire claimed frequent or occasional assistance from *unconscious intuitions*. This creative help from some mysterious "unconscious" process has been mentioned by creative people for centuries. The discovery that our right brain is capable of its own independent train of thought beyond our conscious awareness gives us a physical explanation for that process. Most of our waking life is under conscious control of our left brain. When we are blessed with a creative "flash of insight," it usually emerges in a surprisingly complete form. It appears to be the end result of some real "thinking" of which we are not aware. Since we know that the right brain is capable of thought that seems to us unconscious, it is very probable that "flashes of insight" originate in the right brain.

Mozart described his apparently subconscious process of musical composition in a famous letter:[9]

> When I feel well and in a good humor, or when I am taking a drive or walking after a good meal, or in the night when I cannot sleep, thoughts crowd into my mind as easily as you could wish. Whence and how do they come? I do not know and I have nothing to do with it. Those

which please me, I keep in my head and hum them; at least others have told me that I do so. Once I have my theme, another melody comes, linking itself to the first one, in accordance with the needs of the composition as a whole: the counterpoint, the part of each instrument, and all these melodic fragments at last produce the entire work.

When the composition was complete, Mozart often wrote down the notes directly from the musical image in his head. Sometimes, as he wrote out the score, he would even have his wife read to him to occupy his mind so he could more freely write out the notes in his head.[10]

The history of scientific discovery is full of similar examples of breakthroughs that emerge mysteriously from the unconscious. Friedrich von Kekule's famous discovery that benzine and other organic molecules are actually closed chains or rings was the result of a dream in which he saw snakes swallowing their tails. This discovery has been called "the most brilliant piece of prediction to be found in the whole range of organic chemistry."[11] As with most examples of genius, this is not simply a case of good intuition. Kekule's *logical* mind was *open* to the idea and did not just dismiss it as a "dream about snakes." The act of genius requires a real partnership of intuition and logic.

Flashes of intuitive insight almost always involve *recognition of patterns where there are gaps or literal differences.* Just as we may recognize a childhood friend's face even though he has grown up and now has a beard, creative breakthroughs often involve *recognizing* a known principle in disguise.

One of the most famous intuitive leaps in history was Archimedes' discovery of the principle that bears his name. His protector had been given a gold crown that he suspected was adulterated with silver. He asked Archimedes' opinion. Archimedes knew that he could tell whether the crown was pure gold by its weight if only he could measure its volume. As he sat down in his bathtub, the water level rose as he had seen it hundreds of times. This time Archimedes *recognized* that the rising water was the solution to his problem: The volume of water displaced was equal to the volume of his body that was immersed. He was so excited that he jumped out of the tub and ran through the streets crying, "Eureka!" (I have found it!).

This recognition of a disguised relationship was called "bisociation" by Arthur Koestler, because it amounts to finding a hidden relationship between two seemingly unrelated pieces of knowledge. The large gap that has to be filled makes logical thinking useless in finding the solution, just as logical deduction is useless in recognizing your bearded friend's face.

The Creative Process

Studies of creative thinking that predate our present knowledge of left- and right-brain thinking have generally come up with results that are confirmed and clarified by our new knowledge. For example, in a 1945 book titled *The Art of Thought*, G. Wallas broke the creative process down into four stages: preparation, incubation, illumination, and verification. The *preparation* stage consists of gathering relevant information and narrowing the problem until the obstacles are visible. *Incubation* is a period in which the unconscious processes of the mind seem to work on the problem. During this time, it is permissible to think occasionally about the problem, but generally there should be no pressure for a solution. The *illumination* stage may come spontaneously or as a result of conscious effort. This is where intuition and insight produce possible solutions to the problem. Finally, in the *verification* stage the intuitive solutions are logically tested for validity, then organized and elaborated into a finished solution.

These four stages apply to the problem as a whole, and also to the various subproblems into which most problems naturally divide. Effective thinkers learn to interweave the four stages of thought so that while one problem is in the preparation stage, another can be "stewing" in the incubation stage.

The first and last stages of this process are well-defined left-brain tasks that we learn to do in school. The middle two stages are not so easy because they really involve "unconscious" processes. If one can just learn to let the left brain do other work or stand aside during these stages, the right brain will often fill the gap. The idea is to be aware of the problem and open to an intuitive solution. Creative people learn to trust their intuition at this stage and let the ideas flow. Sketching and diagramming thoughts and other nonverbal thinking aids can help disengage verbal thinking. By using nonverbal thinking to *generate* ideas and verbal thinking to *verify* them, one can improve creativity. Since each kind of thinking has its own strengths and weaknesses, the idea is to use the appropriate one for the task at hand. As the French poet Paul Valéry wrote: "It takes two to invent anything. The one makes up combinations; the other one chooses. . . ."[12]

This synergistic relationship between the left and right brains is the real basis of creativity. The very freedom from logic and structure that makes visual thinking so effective for *generating* ideas makes it unable to evaluate them logically. Since many of the ideas produced by illumination truly "don't hold water" when looked at logically, creativity is equally dependent on the left brain's ability to grasp the value of a good idea when it appears and logically work out the problems it presents.

THE RIGHT-BRAIN
REVOLUTION IN EDUCATION

Thinking in Sensory Images

In this word-oriented world, it is very easy to overlook the fact that we have many other kinds of thought besides verbal thoughts.[1] Thinking, after all, consists of manipulation and rearrangement of *memory images*. The ultimate source of the memory images used in thought is our senses. Since vision is the most information-rich of the senses, visual thinking is extremely important and powerful. The other senses, however, also produce memory images which can similarly be the basis of thought.

We can form mental images of sounds, feelings, and tastes in much the same way as we form a visual image. It is even possible to "think" in these sensory images. For example, a perfume designer learns to think in olfactory (smell) images. Athletes and choreographers learn to think directly in "kinesthetic" (movement) images. They develop a "feel" for certain basic movements. The process of combining them and solving movement problems could be called "kinesthetic thinking." A chef creating a new dish thinks in gustatory (taste) images. This process of combining images from memory and anticipating their result is truly a kind of thinking. A fabric designer uses cutaneous (touch) imagery to combine the feel of various fabrics to create a texture that is just "velvety" enough for a desired effect. A musician thinks in auditory images and can often "hear" a composition before writing it down.

To some degree, all of these kinds of thinking are used in conjunction with the verbal thinking of the left brain. Since the verbal consciousness receives only the *results* of thinking in sensory images, it often seems that the results spring from nowhere. One speaks of "having a feel for" music, sports, art, or whatever as though it is something mystical. In reality the results come from real "thinking" that is outside of the awareness of our left brain. Since only our left brain can talk, it is easy to get the impression that it alone can think.

Why Not Educate the Right Brain?

The two halves of the brain differ mainly in that each does its processing in a different "language." Though they are physically almost identical at birth, they develop their different modes of thought through a sort of "training" process.

The basis of this "training" process is the competitive mechanism that allows only one hemisphere to prevail in a particular task. Since the left hemisphere has a *slight* genetic advantage for hearing verbal sounds, it tends to win the competition in responding to verbal inputs. Each time this happens, the left hemisphere's verbal advantage is increased slightly because of reinforcement. As the child matures, the gulf between the language abilities of the hemispheres widens as a result of this natural "training" process. Since the right hemisphere has less concern for verbal matters, it continues to operate directly on sensory images, while the left becomes more and more specialized for verbal thinking.

When the left hemisphere is removed at infancy, the right hemisphere has no competition, so it develops its own language abilities. The two hemispheres are thus *physiologically* almost identical. Their significant differences in a normal adult are almost entirely a result of the different "training" during childhood.

The amazing plasticity of the brain clearly demonstrates the power that formal education can have over brain development. Education has so far concerned itself mainly with the development of verbal abilities. Since both hemispheres are almost identical physiologically, there is no reason why the same basic principles of education now applied to the left brain can't be applied to the right brain as well.

Educational theory has developed through endless discussions, introspections, and observations in *words*. It is not surprising, then, that the nonverbal side of knowledge has been almost totally ignored.

Yet the fact is that a person's success in the world is largely dependent on how much his intuitive side has *acci-*

dentally developed. While the schools ignore and even discourage intuition, it remains a necessary element of creative thinking and the key ingredient for success in all fields. We have already given numerous examples from science, mathematics, and the arts. But we need not stop there. While minor clerks and bureaucrats get by without much intuition, top business managers and administrators depend on "gut feel" or "intuition"[2] as an important factor in their decision-making. At the top levels, there are just too many gaps and unknowns for purely logical decision-making.

A salesman can take years of courses and even memorize successful sales pitches; but if he doesn't have that "natural feel," he will never make it to the top of his field. The same can be said for teachers, cooks, engineers, lawyers, or any other profession. One can memorize all the facts and even get high grades. Yet there is another kind of knowledge not taught in school, which is also needed for real success. This mysterious "natural feel" or "intuition" is mysterious only because it is difficult to verbalize.

Of course, education has its limits, and our highly refined verbal teaching techniques can't make everyone an "A student" even on verbal subjects. To the same extent that verbal teaching can improve verbal performance, the abilities of the right brain can also be developed by education. However, at present any development of the right brain by education is purely accidental.

Donald Taylor, of Yale University,[3] studied correlations between engineers' grades in the last two years of college

and employers' ratings of their originality. The results
showed a correlation of only .26.* A similar study of fifty-
six physicists gave correlations of only .21.[4]

Since grades are a measure of how well the student
learned what was taught in college, these poor correlations
show that something important was missing from the cur-
riculum. This missing ingredient may well be the development of the right brain's nonverbal thinking abilities.

In another experiment, 267 college students were given a
test designed to measure intuitive thinking ability. When
the results were compared with the student's cumulative
grade point average, virtually no correlation (.048) was
found.[5] The study concluded that "intuitive thinking is
clearly *unrelated to college grades.*"

The Left-Brain Take-over of Education

There is a decadence in the field of higher education
that is the natural result of an ignorance of the "unconscious" side of the brain. A sort of academic dream world
has been created in which purely left-brain thinkers admire
each other's "scholarliness." Many students who earn their
Ph.D.s become so habitually "left-brained" that they are
unable to do anything but become "scholars" themselves.
The system thus feeds itself and becomes more and more
scholarly and less and less intuitive.

One of the highest exemplars of "scholarliness" is the

* Correlation coefficients are an indication of how strongly two functions
are related. A correlation of zero indicates no relationship; a correlation
of one indicates that the two functions are virtually the same.

Shakespearean specialist who spends his career discussing Shakespeare's life and works. While all of Shakespeare's works fit one volume, the books discussing them fill entire aisles in a university library. There are even periodicals dedicated to further the discussion. It is a purely verbal world of verbal discussion of Shakespeare's verbal works. While the scholars appreciate one another's works, there is an air of decadence about the whole thing. For behind Shakespeare's beautiful use of words is an *intuition* that makes the scholars' verbal nit-picking look sad by comparison.

Yet the left-brain take-over of higher education would be much less harmful if it didn't totally dominate the field of elementary education. There is no other field as degree-conscious as education. Pay scales are generally based on a formula that includes the number of academic credits completed. Most policy makers of primary and secondary education have doctor's degrees. The result is a selection process that eliminates intuitive thinkers from high positions in education. People who started out with a good intuitive feel for education often have it "educated out" of them in the process of getting their doctorates.

Most of the educational journals today look more like they are directed at business managers. "Management by objectives" is often used to optimize the educational product. The problem with this approach is that the objectives must be well defined and easily tested. The tendency is thus to optimize memorization of well-defined verbal facts[6] and ignore the more subtle and less easily tested effects of right-brain knowledge.

Can Education Change Itself?

It is unfortunately much easier to identify what is wrong with our educational system than to do something about it. New right-brain-oriented teaching programs, for example, will certainly not solve the problem because the problem goes much deeper than the program level.

The real problem is that the *basic thinking* of the entire educational establishment must be changed before real results can be obtained. A teacher who habitually thinks verbally simply cannot feed the children a course on intuitive thinking. The real patterning must occur day in and day out in the teacher's approach and attitude on all subjects taught. Unfortunately, a teacher's habitual thought patterns are pretty well set. After decades of verbal thinking, it is not easy to change basic thought patterns and simply become intuitive. The real changes are only going to come slowly, as the teachers themselves change.

Fortunately, nonverbal thinking is impossible to ignore in the lower grades because a child's language ability has not yet fully developed. In the first few years of school, there is already a real awareness of the importance of educating children with nonverbal concepts—an obvious need given their difficulty with simple visual and spatial tasks. For example, putting a shirt on right side up requires a certain level of spatial ability. After these basic nonverbal skills are developed, however, the schools essentially stop all conscious effort toward further development.

For most older children the effects of this increasingly

verbal approach are most obvious in creativity, as exemplified by their artwork. As a child progresses through the grades, there is a gradual diminishing of creativity and intuition as his artwork loses its fresh originality and becomes more logical and stereotyped.

Even IQ testing reflects this pattern. The Stanford-Binet IQ test for the younger age levels includes nonverbal problems such as maze tracing and mutilated pictures. At the higher age levels, these problem types are omitted and the test becomes almost completely verbal in content. Lewis Terman, who developed the test, believed that reasoning with verbal concepts was the highest expression of intelligence.[7]

If a child grows up with Einstein's ability to handle complex concepts nonverbally, it is strictly accidental. Even though the school abandons that side of the education by the fifth grade, some people are able to develop their abilities anyway. Just as some school dropouts develop their verbal abilities to a high level without help, the Einsteins of the world have had to develop their nonverbal thinking abilities on their own.

A real reform of the educational system will not occur until *the individual teachers learn to understand the true duality of their students' minds*. With this awareness it becomes only natural to conduct the class in a way that *keeps the attention of both the verbal and the nonverbal minds*.

The split-brain researchers have shown that one hemisphere or the other tends to dominate depending upon which one "feels more strongly" about an answer. These feelings of confidence are reinforced daily in the classroom give-and-take.

The frightening thing is that this competitive balance is so delicate. If the nonverbal mind is ignored, it pays less attention, learns less, and gradually becomes less and less able to compete. What starts out as a slight disadvantage gradually develops into a larger difference in confidence and ability. As time goes by, it becomes increasingly harder to make the nonverbal mind pay attention and participate.

To reverse this trend, teachers must become aware of the nonverbal side of each student. Of course, this is extremely difficult unless the teacher's own right brain is functional. Teachers must learn to *feel* their nonverbal consciousness and to respect intuition and nonverbal thinking. They must avoid relying exclusively on words or formulas in their lectures. Both gestures and pictures are powerful ways to communicate with the nonverbal side of the student.

A teacher who thinks in images finds it hard to explain anything without drawing it or at least using gestures to indicate the images. One example of this on the high school or college level is the study of electromagnetic fields. While it is possible to present the subject entirely with words or formulas, it is much clearer and more useful if a "feel" for the magnetic "lines of force" is communicated as well. This intuitive concept can be demonstrated with a magnet and some iron filings. It is such a powerful concept that Michael Faraday was able to discover most of the principles of magnetism intuitively with it. If a student can develop this "intuitive feel" and also understand the equations that describe the same thing, he will have the basis of real creative thinking.

By having the student use his intuition to "discover" the equations himself, some real practice in left-right synergy can be accomplished in the classroom. There is a kind of order in all of nature that causes the same equations to reappear in seemingly unrelated places. For example, the same kind of *flow* that is observable in water also occurs with heat, electricity, gases, and even magnetic lines of force. All of these can be expressed in equations or visualized.

If we don't get too lost in the equations, *everything* in science fits together and makes sense on an intuitive level. Every educated person should have a "sense of scientific beauty" not captured in equations. This feeling is much like the aesthetic sense of the painter, sculptor, or musician. In fact, the two feelings are one in the same. That is why nature has the same beauty whether we look at it through a telescope or a scanning electron microscope.

Creative Problem Solving

If a child can be encouraged to *make a discovery nonverbally and then verbalize his findings*, he will actually be practicing the creative process. Science and math experiments can easily be set up to encourage this discovery process. When the student learns a concept in this way, there is less need to "memorize it" because he will know it in a deeper, more intuitive way. In addition to exercising his creative powers, the student learns the concept in both a verbal and a nonverbal sense.

The figure below is a simple example of how students can be "set up" to make their own mathematical discoveries. After finding the areas of several rectangles by counting squares, the student is asked to generalize a rule for the area of any rectangle. Finding that the area is the product of the length of the sides is a real discovery, since a pattern observed in several problems must be generalized. The final step is converting the intuition into symbolic form: Area$=a\times b$.

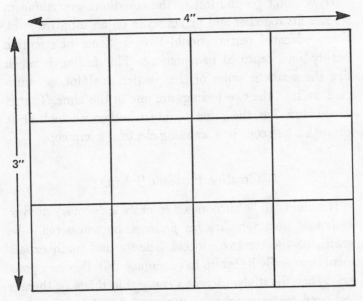

More complex algebraic concepts can similarly be introduced by setting the student up to discover them intuitively.[8] For example, the figure below is a graphical solution to the problem of squaring a binomial: $(a+b)^2=?$ Once the student has drawn a square with the length of each side equal to $a+b$, the answer can be found by simply adding up the areas of the resulting squares and rectangles. When the student writes his result out in equation form, he *discovers* that $(a+b)^2=a^2+2ab+b^2$.

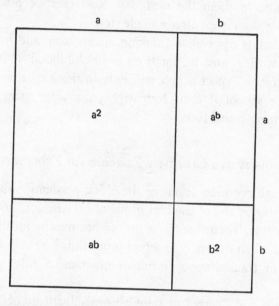

This kind of learning by discovery does more than exercise the student's creative powers. Since the concept is "learned by both sides of the brain," the student gains not only a new formula but an intuitive understanding as well.

Students and teachers must both understand that verbal thoughts involve only half of the brain. There is no reason why children should not be taught the *techniques* of thinking. The idea of incubation, for example, should be understood and used by the students. If they fail to make the proper "discovery" required to learn a new principle, they should be allowed to let the problem "incubate" for a day or two. Even if they immediately make the expected "discovery," they should be encouraged to share any additional insights or extensions of the discovery that may come to them the next day. Real creative problem solving seldom stops after a single step.

The habits of creative thinking are so basic and important that they must be practiced from childhood. It is unreasonable to expect people suddenly to think creatively in graduate school if their formative years were spent just memorizing verbal facts.

Geometry as a Creativity Exercise: An Experiment

Though geometry is one of the oldest academic subjects, it can also be one of the best forms of exercise for the creative process. Theorems to be proven are usually intuitively obvious when drawn. The actual proof thus becomes an exercise in translation of intuitive observation into verbal logic.

Franco and Sperry,[9] of the California Institute of Technology, confirm the crucial role of communications between the hemispheres in the solution of geometry problems. Two of the split-brain subjects[10] who were doing otherwise passing schoolwork were having exceptional difficulty in geometry. To study the hemispheric effects of geometry further, an experiment tested the abilities of five split-brain patients.

The task consisted of feeling with one hand three geometric shapes hidden behind a screen and deciding which one best matched five similar figures that were visible. For example, while looking at five different-sized equilateral triangles, the subject had to feel three triangles and find the one that matched. While none of the three matched exactly, only one had all three sides of equal length. On this particular problem the right brains (left hands) scored only slightly better: 84 per cent vs. 76 per cent.

As the problems got harder, the gulf between the left- and right-hand scores widened: With four-sided figures the scores were 70 per cent vs. 54 per cent. More complex multisided figures increased the gulf to 82 per cent vs. 45 per cent. Finally, when curved (topological) figures were used, the left-brain score dropped to the pure chance (33 per cent) level while the right brain scored 86 per cent.[11]

The left brain did fairly well with the simple Euclidean (triangle) problems because a verbal strategy, like looking for a "medium isosceles triangle," could be used. However, as the forms grew more complex, a verbal strategy became less and less effective. The left brain's performance on the impossible-to-verbalize, topological figures fell to chance level. These same figures were so easy for the right brain that they resulted in the highest score of all! The time required to answer also differed greatly depending on which hand was used: The left-brain responses generally took twice as long and were often accompanied by indications of uncertainty.

Since success in a geometry class requires that visual reasoning be verbalized into logical proofs, it is easy to see why split-brain patients would have great difficulty. Because the right brain cannot communicate its insights to the left, the split-brain patient is forced to depend completely on left-brain thinking. Normal students, who find geometry impossible, may be no better off than split-brain patients: Though they have intact connections between the hemispheres, they may already have such a strong habit of verbal thinking that they are unable to make use of their right brain's abilities.

Thinking and Visual Fields

With little help from the schools, some students seem to pick up naturally the ability to think with both halves of their brain. These students stand out as highly creative and often show an early interest in math and science. Meredith Olson, a teacher of gifted children in Seattle, noticed that these creative students were changing the angle of their heads to the left for verbal tasks and to the right for non-verbalizable tasks. They appeared to be actually using one visual field or another depending on the type of task.

Olson designed an experiment to examine objectively the student's use of visual field.[12] Problem sheets were made up with random sequences of verbal and figural problems arranged vertically down the center of each sheet. A video tape recorder was used to observe the student's face as he solved the problems. Uninformed observers viewed the videotapes and judged whether the students were using their right or left visual field for each problem. When the visual field ratings were correlated with problem types, it was found that 96 per cent of the gifted students' head shifts corresponded to use of the correct visual field:[13] They were using their right visual field for the verbal problems and their left field (right brain) for the spatial problems!

When the same tests were done on students not classified as mathematically gifted or highly creative, the results showed a predominately left-brain approach to *all* problems.[14] It appears that the gifted, creative students were selectively using the appropriate side of their brain, while the noncreative students were habitually using only their left brain. Stronger right-brain development was also confirmed in the creative group by their high scores on the block design test.[15]

Modern Technology and Education

Modern technology has given us tools that are both good and bad for education. Among the good tools are the excellent visual aids that supplement pure verbal presentation. Books filled with pictures and diagrams speak to both sides of the brain. Animation in movies and television dramatically helps students visualize difficult concepts.

Using computers for education has so far had a negative effect because it has encouraged memorization of facts and use of multiple-choice questions. While multiple-choice questions are easily scored objectively, they discourage creativity and intuitive thinking. When the problem is reduced to eliminating three out of four possible answers, the advantages of a right-brain solution are often eliminated.

Facts are easily taught and tested by a machine, but this

is no reason to make them the object of education. Most of the dates, formulas, and other facts learned in school are soon forgotten and can just as well be looked up in a reference book. Real education is what remains after all those facts and formulas are forgotten.

The computer will someday transcend the fact teaching stage to become a powerful tool for providing visualizations of concepts that can be manipulated by the student. Just as driving a car gives us a "feel" unlike any amount of verbal instruction, "playing with" an animated simulation can give a "feel" for other complex concepts.

For example, a microcomputer can be programmed to display graphically mathematical functions with input variables controlled by the student. The student can thus "play with" the equation and actually *see* the effects of increasing x, decreasing y, etc. With this kind of connection to reality, the student's "feel for mathematics" can be intentionally developed by education.

The already popular home video games allow a child to develop a "feel" for rebound ball games by a similar interaction. As the child moves the control levers, he is actually changing the input variables on equations in a microcomputer. The missing element is a display of the equation and the values being used.

It is important to remember that in an intellectual subject like mathematics, isolated intuitive knowledge is of little use if it can't interact with verbal thinking. If a student plays catch with a softball, he may acquire an excellent intuitive feel for the trajectory equation. However, it is of no use to him in mathematics unless that feel is related to the equation in the student's mind. By playing with an *equation* instead of a ball, the same powerful "intuitive feel" can be made useful in mathematics class.

With the trajectory equation graphically displayed on a computer terminal, the student can play with more than just the force and angle of throwing the ball. He can also "play with" the mass of the ball and see its effect on the ball's path. He can even increase the force with which the simulated ball is thrown, to the point where it goes into orbit or escapes the earth's gravity entirely. Since the student always works directly with the equation yet sees real graphical results, the two modes of thinking are taught to work together.

The real power of graphical computer representation of equations is that it can be used even on complex differential equations, calculus, and advanced mathematics courses. Instead of a purely verbal, abstract presentation, the study of math can be turned into a combined exercise in intuition and abstract verbal reasoning.

Imagery and Memory

In spite of all that has been said against the teaching of facts in school, memorization is still crucial in some school subjects. Foreign languages, for example, require large vocabularies to be committed to memory.

Our verbal and visual memories are separate and independent systems. For example, J. P. Guilford, of the University of Southern California, found that there is no correlation between a person's *verbal* fluency and *figural* fluency test scores.[16] In spite of this separation, it is possible to use the powerful abilities of visual memory as an aid in memorizing verbal material.

Professional memory experts are able to do incredible feats by using tricks that involve recoding verbal material into complex visual images. The complex images are easily recalled and translated back into words. Images are more easily remembered if they are very funny, sexy, or bizarre— the kind of thing that would be hard to forget if you actually saw it.[17]

Since our visual memory system is so flexible, it is difficult to remember images in a fixed order. Memory systems have been created to associate images so that, for example, the points to be covered in a speech can be recalled in the proper order. One such system involves placing the images in the rooms of your house. As you walk through in a fixed order, the images are recalled. The act of recall is thus as simple as telling about an interesting experience or dream, in which you walked through your house and saw many strange things.

The superiority of our memory for images was confirmed in an experiment by Allen Paivio, of Canada. Pictures, concrete nouns, or abstract nouns were flashed on a screen for only ¹⁄₁₆ second at five-second intervals. The subjects were asked to write down what they saw. The experiment was done with two different kinds of instructions to the subjects: *Incidental* memorization was tested by telling the subjects that the purpose of the experiment was to see if they could identify the briefly flashed words and pictures. *Intentional* memorization was tested by instructing the subjects to both write and memorize what they saw. In both cases half of the subjects were tested for recall after five minutes and the other half were tested one week later.

The results[18] show that recall of pictures was so much better than recall of abstract words that *the incidental recall score for pictures after one week was actually better than the recall of intentionally memorized abstract words after five minutes!* Interestingly, about 75 per cent more concrete words were remembered than abstract words, the reason probably being that concrete words can evoke mental *images* of the things they represent. Abstract words (such as "moral," "theory," "ego," "ability") evoke no such images, so our memory of them is not aided by our visual memory.[19]

In a classroom situation, learning can be greatly improved if verbal material is reinforced by imagery. When we read or write prose, there should be a parallel flow of imagery in the mind. Since imagery is a slower, more holistic process, the images do not follow the words on a one-to-one basis. When reading prose, images are related more to the feel of entire passages rather than to individual words. In good writing, the basic ideas, "feel," and organization of the story are manipulated in the form of images. Words are then created to express these images. Understanding and appreciating prose should be the reverse of this process: The words should evoke images. These images are what we recall and recode into words when we retell a story. Verbatim memorization is much more difficult because it consumes so much memory space. Since "a picture is worth a thousand words," image memory represents

much more efficient storage. The problem with volumi-
nous note taking in class is that it interferes with the imaging process that could store the same *concepts* much more
efficiently. Diagrams with only key words, rather than complete sentences, make it possible to use words as a memory
aid without obscuring the structure of the concepts themselves.

Imagery can be used to enhance the learning of individual word definitions[20] by having the student create a picture in his mind that represents the word. Again bizarre or
dramatic images are more effective than boring ones. The
Lozanow method of foreign language instruction, developed in Bulgaria, combines imaging with relaxation exer-
cises and positive suggestion to produce a spectacular accel-
eration of learning.[21] When imaging is used with the study
of new vocabulary words, a meaning beyond the purely verbal is learned. Foreign language students often learn words
without having a "feel" for them. When words are imaged
as they are learned, they evoke more than just a verbal
translation when we hear them.

Experiencing Nonverbal Consciousness

One of the greatest barriers in teaching highly verbal
people how to use their right brain is that they cannot be-
lieve that they have a nonverbal consciousness. Three thousand years ago the Eastern men of wisdom discovered techniques for silencing verbal thoughts, thereby tapping
nonverbal consciousness. In China this way was known as
tao, in India as yoga, in Japan as Zen. All three disciplines
are the polar opposite of verbal Western intellectualism.

The philosophies behind these disciplines often represent an extreme denial of the left brain, which is as one-sided as our denial of the right. Some of the techniques they have developed, however, could be used to give students a taste of pure right-brain consciousness. If the Oriental approach was applied to classes in art, dance, music, and sports, it would provide an excellent antidote for the overdose of verbal thinking in the schools today. The present-day approach to these classes grows gradually more verbal after the fourth grade. By the end of high school, the verbal content is often so great that music and art theory courses almost resemble physics courses. Instead of learning to "think musically" or "think visually," the students memorize verbal rules to pass verbal tests.

In one study at Columbia University,[22] dichotic listening tests were given to people with four years or more of musical training and to untrained listeners. The untrained listeners showed the normal left-ear advantage for melodies, while the musically educated showed a right-ear advantage. It appears that today's music education courses change music listening from a right-brain activity into a left-brain one.

One of the reasons for the overly verbal approach to the arts in schools is that the standards (degrees, tests, etc.) developed for teachers of verbal subjects are often applied to teachers of the art and movement courses.

There has been a recent trend to eliminate art, music, and physical education requirements to "make room" for more academic subjects. The problem with this idea is that *mental fatigue* is what really limits the number of academic subjects that can be handled. If art and movement courses are taught in a right-brain manner, they can act as a "rest period" for the left brain. The mental recuperation provided by pure right-brain activities can be useful to the student long after he finishes school. Time spent in purely nonverbal activity helps to keep that channel open and prevent the habit of thinking only verbally from developing.

Probably the most applicable form of the Oriental disciplines is the Japanese Zen tradition in practical and fine arts.[23] Preparatory ceremonial ritual is used to silence the mind. Importance is placed on the reduction of words and thinking to the barest minimum. The emphasis is on total feeling through organic body gesture. By practice and repetition, the craft is mastered until it flows without any conscious effort.

Since first-graders can easily approach art and movement nonverbally, the problem is simply to keep this natural ability alive. The educational system destroys this natural ability by gradually changing the child's thinking to verbal thinking in *all* areas. By keeping art and movement classes nonverbal, the child's nonverbal awareness and abilities can continue to develop along with his verbal abilities.

Though today's educational system is terribly unbalanced toward the verbal-analytical approach, it is important that we don't sell that approach short. Man tried the totally right-brain approach for hundreds of thousands of years with no real progress. The real emergence of man started only a few thousand years ago when he started augmenting his intuition with written language. Man's highest achievements are a result of using the full power of *both halves* of the brain together.

Intuition, by itself, has definite limitations. Optical illusions are good examples of how our intuition can mislead us: Our intuitive perception tells us one thing; but careful analytical measurement tells us another. While we can intuitively estimate some things with uncanny accuracy, intuition can also greatly mislead us. For example, try estimating how thick a piece of tissue paper, $\frac{1}{500}$ of an inch thick, would be if it could be folded in half twenty-eight times. We can calculate the answer as $2^{28} \div (500 \times 12) = 44,739$ feet, which is considerably higher than Mount Everest! In spite of the power of intuition, it has definite limitations.

Investigations into the poor IQ scores of disadvantaged children have shown that much of their trouble is that they *guess* at the answers.[24] Great care must be exercised in teaching children how to use their intuition in thinking. Intuition is useful for bridging difficult gaps in a problem, but often there are no gaps to bridge. In any case, the ideas generated by intuition must be tested by logic in most situations. The important thing is to learn to make full use of both kinds of thinking *appropriately*. All revolutions have a tendency toward excess; let us hope that the right-brain revolution can do *more* than replace our present overemphasis on the left brain with an overemphasis on the right.

Chapter 5

THE INNER SPORTS REVOLUTION

Inner Tennis

In 1974 tennis pro Tim Gallwey wrote *The Inner Game of Tennis,* an immediate best seller. Gallwey went on tour holding tennis clinics before massive coliseum audiences, hosted an Inner Tennis television series, and eventually expanded the concept to include "inner skiing."

Though the inner-game approach to sports makes no reference to the left and right brains, it is a sound application of the discoveries we have been discussing. Gallwey's idea is that each person's mind contains a verbal "Self 1" and a separate, unconscious "Self 2," which actually plays the game. The basis of the inner game is to get Self 1 to stand aside and let Self 2 play the game. The inner-game instructional technique uses verbal instructions where useful, but avoids verbal descriptions of the actual movements. Visual and kinesthetic images are used to teach a nonverbal understanding of the required movements.

Gallwey's excellent understanding of our two separate

selves is developed, not from brain research, but from simple observation of his tennis students and himself. To quote Gallwey:[1]

. . . Most players are talking to themselves on the court all the time. "Get up for the ball." "Keep it to his backhand." "Keep your eyes on the ball." "Bend your knees." The commands are endless. For some, it's like hearing a tape recording of the last lesson playing inside their head. Then, after the shot is made, another thought flashes through the mind and might be expressed as follows: "You clumsy ox, your grandmother could play better!" One day I was wondering who was talking to whom. Who was scolding and who being scolded. "I'm talking to myself," say most people. But just who is this "I" and who the "myself"?

Obviously, the "I" and the "myself" are separate entities or there would be no conversation, so one could say that within each player there are two "selves." One, the "I," seems to give instructions; the other, "myself," seems to perform the action. Then "I" returns with an evaluation of the action. For clarity let's call the "teller" Self 1 and the "doer" Self 2.

Gallwey relates his discovery that nonverbal demonstrations were more effective in correcting students' bad habits than verbal descriptions. The key to better tennis instruction is to concentrate on teaching the nonverbal Self 2 and improving the relationship between the verbal and nonverbal selves. If Self 1 is always yelling at and criticizing Self 2, performance is bound to suffer. Indeed, peak performance, according to Gallwey, usually occurs when the verbal self completely stands aside.

. . . Reflect on the state of mind of a player who is said to be "hot" or "on his game." Is he thinking about how he should hit each shot? Is he thinking at all? Listen to the phrases commonly used to describe a player at his best: "He's out of his mind"; "He's playing over his head"; "He's unconscious"; "He doesn't know what he's doing." The common factor in each of these descriptions is what might be called "mindlessness." There seems to be an intuitive sense that the mind is transcended—or at least in part rendered inoperative. Athletes in most sports use similar phrases, and the best of them know that their peak performance never comes when they're thinking about it.

Clearly, to play unconsciously does not mean to play without consciousness. That would be quite difficult! In fact, someone playing "out of his mind" is more aware of the ball, the court, and when necessary, his opponent. But he is not aware of giving himself a lot of instructions, thinking about how to hit the ball, how to correct past mistakes or how to repeat what he just did. He is conscious, but not thinking, not *over-trying*. A player in this state knows where he wants the ball to go, but he doesn't have to "try hard" to send it there. It just seems to happen —and often with more accuracy than he could have hoped for. The player seems to be immersed in a flow of action which requires his energy, yet results in greater power and accuracy. The "hot streak" usually continues until he starts thinking about it and tries to maintain it; as soon as he attempts to exercise control, he loses it.

To test this theory is a simple matter, if you don't mind a little underhanded gamesmanship. The next time your opponent is having a hot streak, simply ask him as you switch courts, "Say, George, what are you doing so differently that's making your forehand so good today?" If he takes the bait—and 95 percent will—and begins to think about how he's swinging, telling you how he's really meeting the ball out in front, keeping his wrist firm and following through better, his streak invariably will end. He will lose his timing and fluidity as he tries to repeat what he has just told you he was doing so well.

Though Gallwey makes no mention of the physical location of Self 1 and Self 2, it is clear that they are actually the left and right hemispheres of the brain. While either hemisphere is capable of controlling both sides of the body, only the right hemisphere is capable of instantly reacting to the many simultaneous spatial variables of a tennis game. The split-brain experiments showed us that the hemisphere that feels most strongly that it can handle a problem will tend to take control. By emphasizing nonverbal knowledge of tennis skills, the right brain is given a clear competitive advantage.

The opposite of the inner-game approach is to fill the student with verbal descriptions of theoretically proper movements. The student's left brain thus "thinks it knows a lot" and tends to interfere with natural movements.

One of the techniques Gallwey uses to disengage the verbal self during practice is distraction: While the ball is hit back and forth, the student is asked to say "Bounce!" whenever the ball bounces and "Hit!" whenever it hits a racket. This verbal task keeps the verbal consciousness occupied and ensures that body and racket movements stay under right-brain control.

Another technique for quieting the verbal consciousness

is to concentrate on breathing and actually count your breaths. Singing a familiar song to yourself also does the job. Though a part of the right brain may be involved in the automatic singing of a song, it apparently doesn't interfere with right-brain control of your tennis. Singing *does*, however, interfere with verbal thoughts. You can prove this to yourself by trying to sing a song and simultaneously think verbal thoughts (no fair thinking during pauses!).

All of these techniques for quieting verbal thoughts are, of course, slightly distracting. They are useful for breaking bad habits, but the real key to top performance is to be able to play instinctively in a nonverbal mode. If this is carried too far, you may find that you lose track of the score and miss some chances in court position strategy. Between points there is often time to sneak in a little logical thinking; but there simply isn't time for logic during fast play.

Is Self 2 the Right Brain?

Though the verbal consciousness of Self 1 clearly corresponds to our left brain, Self 2 is slightly more complex. When we speak of the left and right brains, we are referring to the cerebral cortex—that portion of the brain that is highly developed only in higher mammals. The cortex actually rests on top of the smaller reptilian brain, the cerebellum, and the spinal cord. These lower parts of the brain also have nonverbal knowledge in that they handle basic elements of movement and balance.

Since patients with right-brain damage often cannot

handle simple spatial relationships such as finding their way about or dressing themselves properly, it is clear that the right brain is needed to program the complex movements of tennis. When the ball bounces with a certain amount of spin and is deflected slightly by wind, the player must run across the court and swing the racket at just the right time and angle to return the ball to an inconvenient location for the opponent. Truly this is a marvel of instant calculation that requires the intelligence and parallel processing of the right brain.

A verbal description of such a task is, at best, a gross oversimplification. Since experimental evidence has consistently shown that left-brain performance is related to "ease of verbalization," it is clear that left-brain control will result in very poor performance. One simply has to watch a "stiff" tennis student trying to do a serve to verbal instructions to see left-brain programming in action. Instead of a single smooth flow of movements, the left-brain approach is a sequence of verbalized submovements that don't flow together smoothly. Few players actually play the game in this stiff mode, so the bad effects of Self 1 are more likely to be momentary interferences than a complete take-over of control.

Though Gallwey describes Self 2 as "the unconscious doer" he is aware that it is not unconscious, but simply has a different kind of consciousness. The Self 2 that learns nonverbally to execute smooth, natural strokes is actually a combination of the right brain and the motor skills and balance in the lower parts of the brain.

One of the key concepts in inner tennis is the development of a good relationship between Self 1 and Self 2. A common symptom of a bad relationship between the two selves is the cursing and name-calling that often occur after a bad shot. The verbal consciousness thinks that it knows better how the shot should have been done, so it actually gets angry at the mistakes it sees. The result is tension and poor performance by Self 2.

Just as a parent can make his child incompetent by continually calling him stupid, Self 1 can ruin Self 2's athletic performance with a poor attitude. The ideal relationship is more like a trusting, loving parent who will let the child learn from his own actions and his own mistakes. A key concept of inner sports is thus to *let* Self 2 hit the ball without verbal interference.

Inner Skiing

The inner-sports concept was originally applied to tennis, but the same concepts are applicable to any activity that is best done by the right brain. In 1977 Bob Kriegel collaborated with Gallwey on *Inner Skiing.* They presented "inner-ski weeks" across the country to teach the method to ski instructors. The results were even more enthusiastic than similar programs for tennis.[2]

Skiing is different from tennis because there is no opponent other than the mountain itself. The closest equivalent to losing is falling and hurting yourself. This added element of fear makes it even more difficult for the verbal self to sit back and trust in Self 2. The result is a very obvious demonstration of the relative abilities of left- or right-brain control. There is a tremendous gulf in ease of learning and abilities between people who can trust their right brain with the task and those who cannot.

Most small children can learn to be really "hot" skiers in only one day. As a person matures he learns to depend more and more on verbal analysis and trust "intuition" less and less. As a result the majority of adult skiing students are unwilling to trust their intuitive right brain to handle the task of skiing. Though adults generally have better developed coordination than small children, very few are able to learn skiing in the quick effortless way that children do. Many adults actually spend years in skiing classes accumulating verbal knowledge without ever *really* learning to ski. The inadequacy of the verbal hemisphere to control the subtle movements of skiing is obvious in the jerky movements these people often make as they repeat the instructor's words in their mind.

Some adults are able to learn skiing quickly and effortlessly. It is easy to confirm that this is the result of nonverbal learning by simply asking them verbal questions about their technique. A natural skier may not even know verbally whether he puts weight on the inside or outside ski while turning—yet he obviously knows on a nonverbal level.

By avoiding verbalizations about body movements, inner skiing keeps the verbal mind from thinking it is an expert on things that it should stay out of anyway. To many people the refusal of the instructor to give verbal descriptions is a frustrating experience. After years of conditioning by the schools it is difficult to put the verbal mind in the back seat.

Verbal instructions are used by inner-skiing instructors primarily to focus the attention on the proper things. For example, the instructor may ask the students to focus their attention on the relative distribution of body weight on the skis. Learning then occurs by a feedback process as the student tries strategies and finds which ones work best. Without this awareness and feedback, there would be little learning. Words are used to set up natural learning experience and to focus the attention on the relevant feedback.

The skiing equivalent of the "Bounce!" "Hit!" technique in inner tennis is to have the student verbally call out numbers to indicate the angle his skis make with the snow at any moment. Besides keeping the verbal mind occupied, this helps focus attention on the angle of the skis. Other tricks for quieting the mind like repeating a word or phrase or singing to yourself have also proven effective.

All good skiers have experienced times when their abilities seem to transcend their normal limitations and they practically fly down the mountain. Invariably when they look back on their state of mind during such a run, it is clear that their mind was completely free of verbal thoughts, and their memory has a strange fragmented quality like a series of snapshots. This is the nonlinear memory of the right brain's holistic processing. The super performance is a result of the right brain's healthy adrenalin reaction to fear.

An equally common reaction occurs when fear causes the left brain to lose confidence in the right brain's ability and seize control. When this happens, the skier's performance completely falls apart and his mind fills with verbal thoughts. After such an experience, the skier usually finds that he has a nice linear memory of the entire nightmarish run.

The important thing in the inner-sports approach is that teaching programs are being tried that take into account the dual nature of our consciousness. The results of these programs demonstrate the potential of this new knowledge and also the difficulties in implementing it. Many people have had exceptionally good results with the inner-sports methods (the author included), but many people have also been disappointed.

The real problem is that you can't change a lifetime of thought patterns in a single lesson. After years of schooling in how to approach everything verbally, many adults simply can't let go of the verbal approach. Another problem is the instructors themselves: After years of teaching verbally, many can't break the habit.

When a *good* inner-sports teacher has a student who already has some confidence in the nonverbal approach, the results can be fantastic. The amazing difference between the quick results under these conditions and the normal ski student's gradual progress in conventional classes clearly demonstrates the human potential that is wasted by our present overly verbal educational system.

Chapter 6

LATERALIZATION AND LANGUAGE PROBLEMS

Development of Lateralization

The human mind is so complex and diverse that any simple generalization about its operation is completely accurate only for the mythical "average person." The simple verbal-nonverbal division of the two halves of the brain is really an oversimplification: While it is a useful model for analyzing modes of thought, it actually represents the theoretical ultimate in lateralization (left-right separation of function).

In real people there is a tremendous diversity of brain organizations[1] with varying degrees of lateralization. At one extreme are the adults who had one hemisphere removed at infancy: They have both verbal and nonverbal thoughts coexisting in a single hemisphere and therefore no lateralization. A normal adult with two hemispheres could theoretically develop both hemispheres in this way with all functions duplicated in each. This would represent the theoretical extreme of no lateralization. The opposite extreme would be a completely lateralized person with a purely verbal left hemisphere and a purely nonverbal right. Most people fall somewhere between the two extremes, having an intermediate degree of lateralization. Some functions exist in both hemispheres while others are present only in one or the other. Some functions may actually be organized such that they require help from both hemispheres.

Since each person's brain is organized in a slightly different way, each person has a unique personality and pattern of abilities. To some degree brain organization is genetically determined, but environmental influences (including education) have a great influence also. The infant hemispherectomy patients demonstrate the tremendous amount of reorganization that is possible to circumvent damaged areas. It is also possible that many people have unique brain organizations that are a result of compensation for minor brain damage that has gone undetected since birth.

The genetic programming for lateralization of the brain is obvious from the moment of birth. Left-hemisphere dominance is demonstrated by one experiment that kept track of the direction one hundred healthy babies held their heads while lying on their backs. It was found that the heads were turned to the right 88 per cent of the time and to the left only 9 per cent of the time.[2] Newborn babies also show a much stronger EEG electrical response from their left hemisphere after speech sounds. Nonspeech sounds give an opposite effect—evoking more response from the right hemisphere.[3]

The neural connections between the left and right hemispheres are incompletely developed in a newborn baby, so his hemispheres are almost as separate as those of a split-brain patient. The maturation (myelination) of these connections is a gradual process, which is mostly completed by the age of six.[4] During this maturation process the left-right organization established is very sensitive to environmental influences.

Although right-handed adults very seldom lose the ability to speak after right-brain injury, children under the same conditions have about a 30 per cent chance of speech loss.[5] It thus appears that some children go through a phase in which speech is represented in both sides of the brain. As these children mature, their right brain more and more leaves speech entirely to the left brain. In the majority of children, speech expression is a purely left-brain function from the beginning.

Proper development of brain lateralization for speech requires a certain amount of exposure to language. In one bizarre case[6] of child abuse, a thirteen-year-old had grown up completely isolated from speech or noise. Her parents never spoke to her and actually punished her if she made any sounds. The result of this deprived verbal environment seems to have been a permanent atrophy of the left-brain functions. While the child had a well-developed spatial ability, language development was poor even after much training. Dichotic listening tests showed an extremely strong left-ear (right brain) advantage for both verbal and nonverbal sounds—in spite of her perfect hearing. Apparently only the child's right brain received enough stimulation to develop normally.

Another indication of the effect of environmental stimulation on brain lateralization is found in deaf children.[7] When a line drawing is flashed into view, normal children show a stronger electrical signal (evoked response) from their right hemisphere. Deaf children with no formal language show no such difference.

Lateralization and Reading Ability

One of the most important skills in our modern society is fluent reading ability. Since written language is such a recent development in evolutionary terms, it is not surprising that there are some otherwise viable brain organizations that are not effective for reading. Dyslexia (reading disability) affects as many as 5 per cent of all school-aged boys[8]— but very few girls. Though intelligence is otherwise normal, dyslectics have a problem with reading much like a tone-deaf person has problems with singing.

Dyslectics are often unable to see the difference between words such as "pot" and "top" or letters such as "d" and "b." Often the problem clears up with therapy or simply as the child's nervous system matures. Since Albert Einstein and Thomas Edison were both dyslectic, it is clear that the associated brain organization is not all bad.

Tests consistently show that dyslectics have a different pattern of lateralization than normal readers. Dichotic listening tests show either left-ear dominance for words[9] or reduced right-ear dominance when compared to normals.[10] The amount of right visual field (left brain) advantage for reading flashed words seems to be directly proportional to reading ability. One experimenter found that it varied from 6:1 for gifted readers to 3.5:1 for good readers to only 2:1 for disabled readers.[11] Dyslectics recognize human figures flashed to either visual field equally well, while good readers do better with figures flashed on the left. Another experiment showed that while normal readers can recognize shapes better when they feel them with their left hands, poor readers do equally well with either hand.[12]

All of these experiments indicate that dyslectics are less lateralized than normal readers. Since they appear to have equal spatial ability in their left and right hemispheres, they may be reading whole words as one would recognize a face. While this look-say approach to reading is usually the basis of "early reading" by very small children, it is *not* effective for fluent reading. To read fluently, one must break the words down into phonetic elements. This approach makes it possible to sound out unfamiliar words and to spell correctly.

Dyslexia thus seems to be a problem of inappropriate strategy. Most children make a natural transition from look-say, early reading to phonetic, fluent reading. Dyslectics are often late-maturing boys who are not ready to make that transition with the rest of their class. They therefore stay with the holistic approach long after normal readers have switched to phonetic analysis. As the reading and spelling get more difficult, they are more and more left behind by their inappropriate strategy.

Therapists are primarily using two approaches for dyslexia:[13] One is to change the child's incorrect strategy by giving him heavy individual phonics drills until he develops enough skills to rejoin a normal class. The other approach is to leave the strategy alone and teach the child to focus more carefully on whole words without phonics. By having the child trace words written by the teacher, he is encouraged to at least pay attention to the details necessary for correct spelling.

The dyslectic child is unlucky to find himself in our phonetic, reading-oriented society. In China, for example, the look-say approach to reading is a must because the words are not phonetic. In a more primitive society, reading ability is unimportant, so the dyslectic would be considered normal.

Inappropriate strategy is the key to many learning problems besides reading. Low-IQ, disadvantaged students often have a bad habit of "shooting from the hip" in answering questions. They are accustomed to using intuition to answer questions that really require sequential-logical analysis. In one experiment it was found that an individual "cognitive therapy" program designed to teach the child how to think analytically caused an average IQ increase of 14.5 points.[14]

Stuttering

Another fairly common language problem related to lateralization is stuttering. About 10 per cent of all children stutter at some stage of their development.[15] In the majority of cases the stuttering clears up naturally in less than a year—probably because of continued development of lateralization.

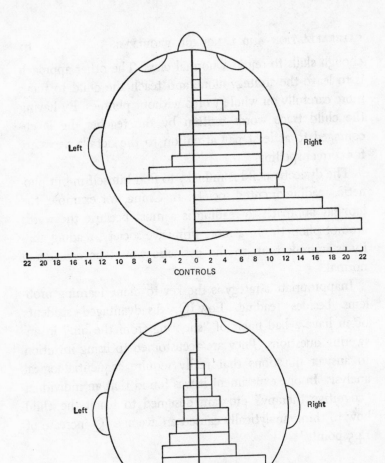

7. *Individual scores for the stutterers and controls (nonstutterers) on the Dichotic Word Test. Bars to the right indicate a right-ear (left brain) advantage for words.*

Around the turn of the century, it was found that about half of all stutterers were left-handed people who had been forced to use their right hand.[16] Since left-handedness is seldom thwarted today, the incidence of adult stuttering is down to about 1 per cent. Both stuttering and dyslexia occur much more often in people who have mixed dominance: for example, people who are right-handed and left-footed.[17] The tendency for mixed dominance seems to be hereditary, so many families have several stutterers or dyslectics in them.

Experimental evidence on the lateralization of stutterers clearly shows that they don't have a well-defined left-hemisphere dominance for language. In one experiment stutterers read words more accurately in the left visual field while normal controls showed the normal preference for words in the right visual field.[18] Figure 7 shows results of a dichotic listening test in which stutterers failed to show the normal right-ear advantage for words.[19] The stutterers scored normally on dichotic tests of *environmental* sounds and monotic (one ear at a time) word tests, so the results were not caused by hearing problems.

Perhaps the strongest evidence of all is contained in a 1966 report by Dr. R. K. Jones.[20] He described four patients who had stuttered since childhood. Each of the four had a damaged speech area on one side of his brain. The damage was recent and unrelated to the stuttering. In all four cases a Wada test indicated that speech was controlled by *both* hemispheres.

After the damaged areas were surgically removed, all four patients *regained normal speech and ceased stuttering.*

A Wada test showed speech was now controlled by only one side of the brain.

In all four patients stuttering was apparently caused by a brain organization with speech on both sides of the brain. Listening to the hesitant speech of a stutterer, it is easy to imagine two separate sources of speech fighting for control. A similar thing occurs when two people try to pass through a narrow doorway at the same moment: They often go through several cycles of starting and stopping ("after you," "no, after you") before they finally resolve the conflict.

Chapter 7

SEX AND LEFT-HANDEDNESS

While sex and left-handedness may seem like strange bed-fellows, they do have something in common when it comes to lateralization. All of the tests that demonstrate left-right differences in brain organization give weaker results when they are given to women and left-handers. The clear implication is that women and left-handed people are less lateralized. We have already seen that problems such as stuttering and dyslexia are related to variations in the lateral organization of the brain. Reduced lateralization has both a good and a bad effect on mental abilities, which may well explain some of the classic differences between men and women. First, however, let us look at left-handedness.

Left-handedness

Between 1932 and 1970 the percentage of left-handed people in the United States gradually rose from 2 per cent to 10 per cent. If we glance too casually at these figures, we can easily get the impression that left-handedness came into existence only recently. In reality, about 10 per cent of the population has been genetically left-handed since the stone age. Social taboos and pressure for conformity have caused many societies to discourage left-handedness by forcing children to learn to be right-handed.

The sudden growth in left-handedness in the last fifty years can be attributed to the discovery that thwarted left-handedness often caused stuttering and emotional problems. As the public became aware of this fact, the true incidence of left-handedness has gradually emerged.

About 70 per cent of all left-handers seem to have language dominance in their left hemisphere—just like right-handers. The other 30 per cent either have language in both hemispheres or have it only in their right hemisphere. Left-handed people thus cover the full range of lateralization possibilities. A series of Wada tests on 262 left-handed and ambidextrous patients had the following results:[1]

Speech in Left Hemisphere   70%
Speech in Both Hemispheres   15%
Speech in Right Hemisphere   15%

Many of the patients with speech in both hemispheres lost different aspects of their language ability, depending on which hemisphere was anesthetized. For example, a patient might have counting ability on one side and naming ability on the other.

Brain damage evidence also demonstrates that left-handers have a variety of brain organizations. In a monumental study of 560 brain-damaged patients (see Appendix I), fifty symptoms were tabulated according to handedness of the patient and side of injury.[2] In right-handed patients, it was found that forty-seven of the fifty symptoms were consistently identified with injuries to a particular hemisphere. For left-handed patients, only four of the fifty symptoms could be identified with a particular hemisphere. It is obvious that any generalizations we make about left-handed people must be interpreted as an *average* of several diverse and unique brain organizations.

When the family backgrounds of the left-handed patients were taken into account, it was found that almost all patients who had language disturbances after right-brain damage had at least one parent or two close relatives that were left-handed. Right-hemisphere speech is therefore almost always an inherited trait. Left-handed people, with no left-handedness in their family, seem to have language entirely in the left hemisphere—just like right-handers. Though adults with left-handedness in the family tend to get aphasia after injury to either side of their brain, they have a much better chance of full recovery. Both halves of their brain seem to have an organization that is compatible with language development.

The Inverted Hand

Jerre Levy[3] discovered a simple test to determine which hemisphere controls the hand when writing. She observed that approximately 60 per cent of all left-handed people write with their hand in the pencil-down, inverted position. Since this is about the same percentage of left-handers known to have language in their left hemisphere, she postulated that the inverted hand position might indicate left-hemisphere language.

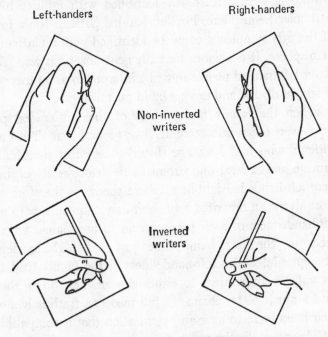

8. *The four possible hand positions for writing. The inverted hand position indicates that control is probably coming from the hemisphere on the same side of the body.*

It appears that when the hand is controlled by the hemisphere on the same side of the body, there is a left-right conflict in visual feedback which makes writing easier with the hand in the inverted position. To test this theory, she classified seventy-three subjects into four groups based on their hand position when writing. She then gave each subject verbal and spatial tests flashed to their left and right visual fields to determine which hemisphere was better at each task.

The results were a dramatic confirmation of the theory: The left-handed subjects who wrote with an inverted hand were found to have the same pattern of left-brain language and right-brain spatial ability as normal right-handers. The lefties who wrote non-inverted and the right-hander who wrote inverted showed the opposite pattern—with language in the right brain and superior spatial ability in the left.

When the differences between the left- and right-hemisphere scores of each group were compared, some other interesting patterns emerged. The lefties who wrote with an inverted hand had a much smaller difference between their left and right visual fields than any of the other groups. Also left- and right-field scores of the women differed by only about half as much as the men. It appears that women and some left-handed people tend to have less of a difference between the abilities of the left and right brains. This reduced lateralization has been confirmed by a large number of other experiments.

Lateralization and Ability

While it is generally agreed that women and some left-handers tend to have more of an overlap of hemispheric abilities, the effect of this reduced lateralization on problem-solving ability has been difficult to show. A large number of studies have shown reduced spatial ability and improved language ability as a result of having language in both hemispheres. An almost equal number of studies have failed to show any difference in ability related to lateralization.

The reason for this confusion is clear if we look at the two hemispheres as a partnership[4] of two minds. The ex-

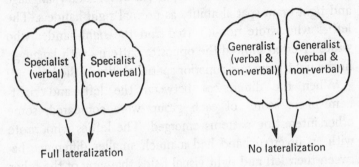

Full lateralization   No lateralization

9. *The two extremes of brain lateralization: two kinds of partnership.*

treme case of lateralization is like a partnership of two narrow specialists: One is adept at verbal and logical thinking while the other is specialized for non-verbal, holistic thinking. When the two specialists attack a problem, one is "out of his field" and therefore of no help, but the other has superior ability to solve the problem. The opposite extreme of lateralization is more like a partnership of two generalists: Each is equally adept at any kind of problem, so the partners can help one another and check each other's work for errors. It is not surprising that this kind of teamwork can often score equally well on intelligence[5] and other tests as the "specialist team" represented by a very lateralized brain.

In fact, one would expect the less lateralized brain to actually score better on fairly routine tasks where speed and accuracy are important. At the outer limits of creativity or difficult problem solving, one would expect the peak performance of specialists to have an advantage. Since there is a need in the world for both kinds of performance, the full spectrum of lateralization that is covered by the normal variation between individuals is important. The world would indeed be a mess if everybody had a brain like Einstein.

Since, on the average, a group of left-handers will be less lateralized than a group of right-handers, we can study the effects of lateralization by comparing the two groups on a task.

As we saw before, it is easier to memorize concrete nouns than abstract nouns, because the concrete nouns evoke a mental image that can be remembered in visual memory. In one experiment[6] the scores of left- and right-handed subjects were tabulated separately. While both groups remembered the concrete nouns better than the abstract, the concrete noun advantage was 36 per cent for the right-handers but only 5 per cent for the lefties. If we think of the more lateralized brain of the right-handers as two specialists, we can see why they remembered more concrete nouns: The images remembered in the right brain helped them remember the concrete nouns, but not the abstract nouns. The less lateralized left-handers tended to use a verbal approach in both hemispheres, causing the imaging advantage of concrete nouns almost to disappear. The left-handers scored slightly higher than the right-handers on the abstract nouns only. This is probably the "two heads are better than one" effect, since both of their hemispheres used the approach most effective for abstract nouns.

The reduced lateralization of some left-handers certainly gives them a different pattern of abilities. However, *most*[7] comparisons of IQ test scores show that the advantages and disadvantages of lateralization pretty well cancel out on the average. Since left-handedness has survived millions of years of evolution, its survival disadvantages must have been balanced by its advantages.

Sex Differences and Maturity

One cannot overlook the fact that women are different from men both physically and mentally. While the physical differences are obvious, the mental differences are so dominated by environmental influences that it is difficult to identify their biological basis.

One clear biological difference between men and women is their rate of maturation: Five months after conception, the female embryo is already two weeks ahead of the male. At birth, a baby girl is about four weeks ahead of a boy in development.[8] A baby girl talks earlier, walks earlier, and reaches puberty and maximum growth two or three years earlier than a boy.[9]

Slow maturation means more time for differentiation and organization of the nervous system. The natural tendency for an infant's left brain to attend to speech sounds has more time to develop before the connections between the hemispheres become functional. Greater lateralization is thus associated with slow maturation.

Deborah Waber, of Boston Children's Hospital, tested this idea by giving lateralization tests to eighty children classified as early or late maturers. She tested two age groups: a young group of ten-year-old girls and thirteen-year-old boys and an older group of thirteen-year-old girls and sixteen-year-old boys.

When their scores were analyzed, a significant difference was found between the early and late maturers. This difference was, in fact, much stronger than the sex difference, which was also noted. The early maturers had significantly better verbal scores while the late maturers had better spatial scores. The older group showed a particularly strong difference.[10]*

The one mental difference between men and women that experts can agree upon is that women are generally superior at verbal tasks and men are superior at spatial ability.[11] It appears that this is a biological difference caused by the faster maturation and reduced lateralization of the female.

Further confirmation that chromosomes can affect lateralization can be found in sex chromosome disorders: In Turner's syndrome, a woman is born with one missing female sex chromosome (XO). Although there is a period of rapid maturation, the adult Turner patient is short and childlike in appearance.[12] Dichotic listening tests show no

* Dichotic listening tests were given to the four groups, and the older late-maturing group was proved to be significantly more lateralized.

consistent lateralization of language in the left brain.[13] Intelligence tests show normal language ability, but severely retarded spatial ability.

The slow maturation of boys also has its disadvantages. The immature brain is very susceptible to damage by high fever. Since boys are in this vulnerable state longer, there is a greater likelihood of developing epilepsy. Stuttering and dyslexia are also much more common in boys than in girls. By getting through the critical developmental period quickly, girls escape many of the problems of improper lateralization.

Testing of Sex Differences

Though many studies both confirm[14] and deny sexual differences based on standardized intelligence test results, the tests are designed to minimize sex differences. To quote David Wechsler,[15] the creator of classic IQ tests:

> . . . in the New Stanford Revision [Test], Terman and Merrill eliminated such tests as they said were "unfair" to one sex or another. And we have done the same. Thus we dropped the Cube Analysis from our battery when we discovered that the mean score for men and women showed systematically large differences in favor of the former.

Intelligence testers generally agree that women excel on tests requiring verbal fluency, speed, and attention to detail while men excel on spatial abilities. J. P. Guilford, who has spent a lifetime testing the various factors of intellect, presents the following list of tests for specific abilities, in which sex differences are generally agreed to occur:[16]

Males Higher	Females Higher
Street Gesalt Completion	PMA Reasoning
G-Z Spatial Orientation	Opposites; Verbal Analogy
G-Z Spatial Visualization	Wechsler Similarities
Porteus Maze	Memory for Figures
Arithmetic Reasoning	Digit Symbol
Match Problems	Memory for Words
Gottschaldt Figures	Word Fluency
	Ideational Fluency
	Expressional Fluency
	Symbol Identities

Males score higher on the type of test that is best solved by holistic right-brain thinking. Of the ten tests in which females score higher, nine are primarily verbal. Certainly "two heads are better than one" applies to all of the fluency tests, so a less lateralized brain organization in which both hemispheres can participate is beneficial (see Figure 9, page 100).

Laterality Experiments

Virtually all of the tests that demonstrate hemispheric specialization in the brain have shown a tendency toward less lateralization in women.[17]

One brain damage study,[18] for example, showed that the average *verbal* IQ scores of thirty-seven women were virtually the same (99.1 vs. 98.9) whether their damage was on the left or the right side. The same study found that a similar group of forty men had a mean score of 83.1 after left-brain damage and 106.8 after right damage.

In a typical experiment[19] on normal people, faces were flashed for 1/50 of a second to the left or right visual field. Female subjects identified the faces on either side with *equal* speed. Males were 1/10 second *faster* than females in their left visual field, but 1/20 second *slower* in their right. When the problem was made easier by flashing the faces for 1/10 second, the sex difference almost disappeared. As we saw before, strong lateralization often shows its advantage only when the problem is very difficult.

In another type of experiment, the subject simultaneously feels a different meaningless shape with each hand. The shapes are hidden from sight. After ten seconds, the subject tries to pick out both shapes on a visual display. One experimenter found that girls did *equally* well with either hand, while the boys did *better* with their left hand (right brain) and *worse* with their right hand. The *total* resulting accuracy was the same for both boys and girls.[20] This is an excellent demonstration of how teamwork between two "specialist" hemispheres can produce results that are equivalent to the results of teamwork between two "generalists."

Why Is There No Woman Beethoven?

One of the disturbing paradoxes about the difference between men and women is that there have been (as yet) no women who are *towering* geniuses. Certainly there are many women who qualify as geniuses, but a towering genius stands head and shoulders above an entire age. Men like Einstein, Leonardo da Vinci, Newton, Beethoven, Bach, Plato, Aristotle, Edison, Darwin, and Shakespeare had abilities that were beyond ordinary genius.

Certainly lack of opportunity or aspiration can account for much of this gap, but the towering genius is such a standout that poverty and persecution have seldom stood in his way. Many women show early promise, achieve recognition and fame in a pattern similar to the towering genius, but that final rise to the sublime level just never happens.

Yet interestingly, at all normal levels of achievement women seem to be equal to men. Their IQ scores and grades in school are the same. Perhaps the answer to this paradox lies in woman's genetically faster rate of maturation and its resultant affect on brain organization. If a woman's brain tends to work like a pair of generalists while a man's is more like a pair of specialists, the mystery may be solved. Since "two heads are better than one," at most normal levels of difficulty females can have a considerable advantage in speed, fluency, and accuracy. At the upper levels of creativity, the two separate modes of thinking described by Einstein become crucial, if a problem is to be solved at all. (Einstein was, incidentally, very late in maturing.)

The kinds of intuitive leaps required at the upper limits of creativity are not compatible with any compromise for generality. Ten thousand jacks-of-all-trades do not equal one Einstein who can think in "visual and muscular" images and then describe the result in words. While Einstein's mind certainly qualified him as a towering genius, he was not successful as a patent clerk. In the more normal range of human activities, Einstein's brain put him at a disadvantage.

Within the normal range of human ability, the number of men and women with a given degree of lateralization is almost equal. The generalization that women are less lateralized than men is like any generalization about people: It can't be applied to *individual* cases. The mere fact of being male is no guarantee that a person is highly lateralized. Many of the inequalities in opportunity for women today result from the mistaken application of generalizations to individuals.

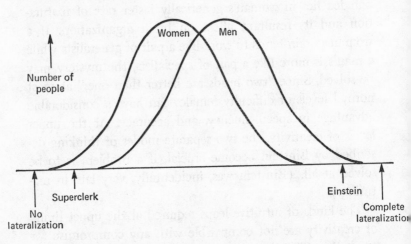

10. *The sex difference in lateralization: a frequency distribution based on age of maturation curves (Hutt 1972, p. 81) and guesstimation.*

Chapter 8

THE BRAIN
IN THE COMPUTER AGE

The Left-Brain Revolution

The past few thousand years have been a time of incredible change for mankind. After billions of years of slow evolution, our powers suddenly grew a millionfold. Though the human brain had evolved to its present size about 250,000 years ago,[1] mankind continued to live in a primitive stone age culture until a few thousand years ago, when a great discovery changed everything. This discovery was no less than a completely new way of thinking.

While mankind had previously responded to the environment in a direct, natural way, they began to discover the power of thinking logically in more abstract terms. The primitive picture writing of 3000 B.C. directly recalled visual images and provided a means of communications across generations. Within a thousand years, this picture writing had evolved into a more abstract hieroglyphic style that still contained pictorial elements. Another short jump toward abstraction brought phonetic alphabets, making it possible to communicate virtually any complex thought in writing.

The tremendous technological progress of the past few thousand years can be attributed to the discovery of the power of logical (left brain) thinking. Stone age cultures still exist in the world today. Their people are biologically the same as you and I. But they have a style of thinking that is distinctly nonverbal. Language to them is valued as a means of communications, but not as a mode of thought.

When writing was discovered, it became possible for each generation to build upon the knowledge of past generations. The logical rules of language became the tools for convincing others of the truth of insights which were often the result of intuitive thinking. In its raw form, intuition is often incorrect. When mankind learned to test intuitive insights with logic, the power of intellect was finally realized. While intuition may be excellent for throwing a rock, it is not effective for estimating the speed and angle of a rocket launch for a particular orbit around the earth. Intuition can be expanded to such a scale only in conjunction with left-brain analysis.

The left-brain revolution expanded our human scope not by replacing right-brain thinking with left-brain thinking, but by joining them in synergism. Since intuitive thinking was already developed, education was originally directed at improving the missing verbal-logical member of the team. Unfortunately, lack of understanding of this partnership has caused education to go too far. Like many successful revolutions, the left-brain revolution has come so far that what is needed is a counterrevolution.

The Computer Revolution

About thirty years ago, another revolution began which will also have an astounding effect on man's capabilities: The computer revolution is essentially an extension of the left-brain revolution. Computers are actually extending our ability to do abstract logical thinking. While computers are hopelessly inadequate for the kind of thinking done by the right brain, they can do most left-brain tasks a million times faster than we can.

This speed advantage is not just theoretical—the computer has already made obsolete many pure left-brain clerical jobs. Any job that only requires following well-defined logical rules is generally better done by a computer. Since computers "think" in digital words, they are subject to the same limitations as people thinking in words: The words must be handled sequentially one at a time, so no flexible process similar to intuition is possible.

While a computer can be programmed to do recognition tasks, it is limited to a very poor one-step-at-a-time strategy. For example, a person can easily recognize printed letters at a glance. A computer can be programmed to recognize letters by analyzing their features one at a time and deducing the letter. If the size of the letter changes, additional program steps can be added to compensate. Further refinements can be added to handle changes in orientation, gaps, or smudges, but each additional variable adds tremendous complications to the program. Even with tens of thousands of program steps, computer recognition is still inferior to one glance by a human being. In spite of its clumsiness, the tremendous speed of a computer often makes it useful even for recognition tasks. But the present concept of a computer will never rival the human right brain.

Experimental "optical computers" have been built[2] which use photographic "memory" and can actually process images holistically. While these are successful in some special recognition tasks, they are far from useful in the sense of a general-purpose computer, as they cannot be programmed to do more general tasks. While present-day computers will grow ever smaller, cheaper, and faster, they will continue to be of the "left brain" type in the foreseeable future.

A New Kind of Synergy

Just as mankind's great leap from the stone age was based on synergy of the left and right brains, progress in the computer age will be based on a new kind of synergy of humans and computers. This new order will require a new kind of thinking and a new emphasis in education. The present verbal emphasis in education has always produced a few creative individuals and a large majority of people who are uncreative, but strong in left-brain skills. This was acceptable because there were a large number of uncreative clerical jobs that required these skills.

In the future, however, those jobs will be done by computers. Education must therefore change its emphasis and concentrate more on development of those skills that are poorly done by computers. Development of creativity and holistic thinking ability should have top priority. While routine calculation skills are no longer important, the left brain's ability to translate intuitive insight into logical verbal sequences remains extremely important.

The synergism of the computer age is a three-way partnership:

COMPUTER $\longleftrightarrow$ LEFT BRAIN $\longleftrightarrow$ RIGHT BRAIN

$\updownarrow$

OTHERS

The right brain has the creativity to bridge gaps and make intuitive breakthroughs, but it cannot test that intuition or communicate it to other people or computers. The left brain has access to the intuitions of the right brain and can test them and convert them to the logical language of computers or other people. The computer augments the abilities of the left brain with perfect accuracy and speed a million times faster than the brain.

Just as the left-right synergy of the human brain lifted mankind from the stone age to the modern world with amazing speed, this new synergy is multiplying the already awesome power of the intellect. As the computer revolution gathers steam, it becomes more and more important for us to fill our role as creator and innovator. With routine and linear thinking left to computers, we will have no more need for "human computers" with atrophied right brains.

If education can redirect its efforts toward a balance between verbal and intuitive thinking it will give us more than technological progress: We will have a world where people can experience both the intellectual and the "feeling" sides of life.

Up the Revolution!

Part II

THE EXPERIMENTAL EVIDENCE

Chapter 9

THE SPLIT BRAIN

In Chapter 1 we quickly reviewed the scientific basis of the right-brain revolution. Now it is time to take a more leisurely look at some of the fascinating experiments and case histories that have shown the way to this new understanding. Through these examples, we can learn to recognize the right brain at work and feel its consciousness in our own head.

The real beginnings of our modern understanding started back in the 1950s when Roger Sperry, of the California Institute of Technology, and his student Ron Myers began split-brain experiments on animals. When they cut all connections between the hemispheres of cats (and later monkeys), they found that the animals remained remarkably normal. Even more exciting, they found that they could train the two hemispheres to respond in opposite ways to the same task![1] For example, the right paw could be trained to push a lever when the animal saw an "X," while the left paw (and left visual field) would ignore the "X" and respond only to an "O."

The next crucial step came in 1962. In a Los Angeles hospital a forty-eight-year-old war veteran began having epileptic seizures so frequently that he hardly recovered from one before another would start. After all other treatments failed, his doctors (Joseph Bogen and P. J. Vogel) decided to try a daring surgical procedure:[2] Since epileptic seizures spread throughout the brain by a kind of electrical chain reaction, they would cut the connections between the hemispheres to localize the seizure to one side of the body.

The results of the split-brain surgery were so good that the operation has since been repeated on dozens of patients. Instead of just reducing the severity of the seizures, the operation stopped them altogether.

After years of research on split-brain animals, the human split-brain patients gave Sperry a golden opportunity. With the help of a student, Michael Gazzaniga, an apparatus was built which allowed separate communications with each of the patient's hemispheres. Words or pictures could be shown, to one hemisphere only, by projecting them briefly on the left or the right side of the screen. Below the screen was a slot for the hands so that objects could be felt with one hand without being seen by the other hemisphere.

In the example illustrated in Figure 11, the subject retrieves a pencil with his left hand after the word "pencil" is flashed on the left side of the screen. Though the subject has already retrieved the pencil, he will still verbally insist that he saw nothing because his verbal left brain did indeed see and feel nothing.

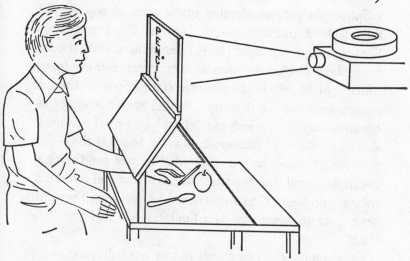

11. *The classical split-brain experiment: While the subject stares at a spot in the center of the screen, a word or picture is flashed on one side of the screen only. In the example shown, only the patient's right hemisphere will see the word "pencil." He will therefore be verbally unable to indicate what he saw, but his left hand will be able to select the pencil from the group of objects.*

If we now flash a word on the right side, the subject can not only pick it out with his right hand but name it and describe it as well. If different words are flashed simultaneously on the left and the right, the subject will pick what he saw on the left with his left hand and name what he saw on the right without being aware of any conflict. When asked about why the left hand picked something else, he may answer with something like "Well, I must have done it *unconsciously*."[3]

Split-brain patients develop subtle ways of coping with
their lack of communications between the hemispheres.
For example, if the right (mute) hemisphere hears the left
hemisphere give an incorrect answer, it can cause a frown
which will be felt by facial nerve connections to the left
hemisphere* causing it to try a second guess.[4] Another interesting way the patient can "cheat" is this: If a word is
flashed on the right side and he is asked to select the object
with his left hand, he can name what he sees and the right
hemisphere will *hear* the name of the object and retrieve it
with no problem. Certainly tricks like this help the split-
brain patients overcome their limitations in real-life situations.

Occasionally the two minds in one head disagree about
what to do. For example, Sperry tells this story about the
first split-brain patient:[5]

> . . . while the patient was dressing and trying to pull on
> his trousers the left hand might start to work against the
> right to pull the trousers down on that side. Or, the left
> hand, after just helping to tie the belt of the patient's robe,
> might go ahead on its own to untie the completed knot,
> whereupon the right hand would have to supervene again
> to retie it. The patient and his wife used to refer to the
> "sinister left hand" that sometimes tried to push the wife
> away aggressively at the same time that the hemisphere of
> the right hand was trying to get her to come and help him
> with something.

* Both hemispheres have nerve connections to the center of the body,
so faces and emotional reactions can often be "felt" by the sensory
nerves in the opposite hemisphere.

The emotional responses of the right hemisphere can affect full facial expressions, even the tone of one's voice, without the left hemisphere knowing what is happening. For instance, Sperry flashed a picture of a nude woman on the left side of the screen. The subject, a young woman, made an embarrassed smile but insisted she saw nothing. When the nude was again flashed, she blushed, giggled, and even hid her face in embarrassment. When pressed to explain why she was laughing, she replied: "I don't know . . . nothing . . . oh, that funny machine."

One of the most exciting findings of the split-brain experiments is the discovery that each separated hemisphere has its own stream of conscious awareness. To quote Sperry:[6]

> . . . in the split-brain syndrome we deal with two separate spheres of conscious awareness, i.e., two separate conscious entities or minds running in parallel in the same cranium, each with its own sensations, perceptions, cognitive processes, learning experiences, memories, and so on.

Since the split-brain patients appear so normal after their surgery, much of what we consider normal behavior is possible without any interaction between the hemispheres whatsoever.

Even Roger Sperry was amazed at how normal the split-brain patients appear to the casual observer. To quote Sperry:[7]

> . . . (L.B.), a boy of thirteen, was talking fluently on the morning following the surgery and was able to recite the

tongue-twister, "Peter Piper picked a peck of pickled pep-
pers . . . etc." He also had recovered already his former
personality and sense of humor and was passing off face-
tious quips to the doctors and nurses on the ward about
having such a "splitting headache" that morning. . . . He
has been able to return to public school after having lost
one year, and is reported to be doing passable work even
though he had long been only a D student before surgery.

This improvement in mental performance after a split-
brain operation is not unusual. Another patient's full-scale
IQ jumped from 92 before the operation to 103 after his
brain was split.[8] This should *not* be taken to mean that we
would all be better off with a split-brain operation! The
poor performance of both patients before their operations
could easily have been caused by the mental stress of their
frequent epileptic seizures. The important fact is that good
test performance is possible even though the connections
between the hemispheres have been cut.

The Abilities of the Right Brain

If the left brain alone can appear so normal, then what is
the purpose of the right brain? Split-brain patients give us
an excellent chance to answer this question because we can
separately test the abilities of each of their hemispheres. For example, the relative abilities of the right
and left hemispheres to deal with fragmented data can be
accurately measured in split-brain patients by simply comparing the test scores of their left and right hands. In one
experiment, the subjects were asked to feel a fragment of a

Plexiglas circle with one hand while looking at three different sizes of complete circles. When the subject decided which circle size matched the partial circle he was feeling, he withdrew his hand and pointed to the circle chosen.

The results showed that the right brain (left hand) has a significant advantage in this kind of task: The average score for five split-brain patients was 61 per cent with the right brain (left hand) and only 33 per cent with the left brain. Since there were only three circle sizes, the 33 per cent score of the left brain is identical to what would be expected by pure chance. In the words of the experimenter:[9]

> The general failure of the right hand even to score substantially above chance level in most cases suggests a basic incompetence of the left hemisphere in this kind of task.

While the left brain was shown to be quite accurate if the fragment was more than half of a full circle, *it was unable to see the connection between smaller fragments and complete circles of the same size.*

Another experiment[10] that strongly demonstrates right-brain superiority is illustrated in Figure 12. In this case the subject looks at a "shattered" drawing of a geometric shape and tries to match it to one of three solid shapes which he feels with one hand.

When this test was given to seven split-brain patients, it was again found that only the right brain (left hand) could handle the problem. While the average left-hand score on the test was 85 per cent, the right-hand scores were only slightly above the level expected by chance. Since the left

Figure 12

hemisphere is so totally baffled by fragmentary information, it appears that when normal people solve such problems they must be calling on the abilities of their right brain. As the right brain by itself has very poor logic and language ability, most creative problem solving requires integration of both the left and the right brains' unique abilities. The split-brain patient, of course, is unable to use the left and right brains together because all connections have been cut between the hemispheres. The fact that they appear normal in day-to-day life simply indicates how little creativity is required in the routine of normal life.

Attentiveness and the Hemispheres

Though the split-brain patients essentially have two minds in one body, they seldom have any problem with conflicting actions. The reason for this is that the brainstem arbitrates by controlling the *attentiveness* of the left and right hemispheres. When we are asleep, neither side of the brain is attentive, but when we are awake, one hemisphere or the other is primarily energized by the brainstem. Though the left brain is generally in control in any verbal situation, the right hemisphere is quite capable of winning the competition for control if it "feels more confident" that it has the answer to the problem.

The two hemispheres are like two separate people with differing talents, where only one of the two is allowed to answer each question. Ideally, the hemisphere best qualified to take charge will answer each question.

This effect was demonstrated very clearly on five split-brain patients[11] by flashing composite words on a screen (see Figures 13a and b) and noting whether they responded to the right or the left half of the word. For example, if "deon" is flashed on the screen, the left brain sees "-on" and the right brain sees "de-." When the patient is asked to indicate which word he saw, his left brain would choose "noon" while the right would choose "deed." The response given thus indicates which side of the brain is answering.

When the subjects were asked to match the "word" on the screen to one of three *words*, 93 per cent of the responses came from the *right* brain. When they were asked to match the "word" to one of three *pictures*, the results reversed to 90 per cent *left*-brain responses.

This dramatic reversal of results from such a seemingly small change in the experiment can be explained as follows: The right brain had a strong advantage in matching the fragmented words to complete words by simply looking for similar *patterns*. When half words had to be matched to pictures, this strategy broke down because there was no

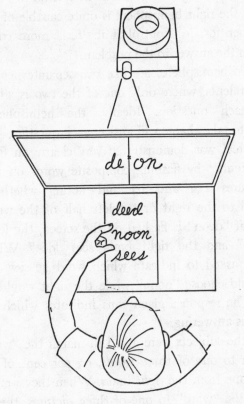

13a. *Experiment favoring pattern matching. Subject's choices:*
    deed (right brain) 93%
    noon (left brain) 6%
    sees (error) 19%

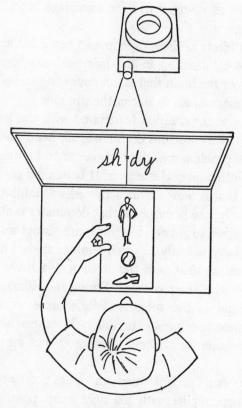

13b. *Same experiment except that words must be read. Subject's choices:*

lady (left brain)   90%
ball (error)   6%
shoe (right brain)   4%

longer any pattern similarity. Since the left brain read the half words as words, it had the advantage in relating them to pictures.

The subjects in these experiments never felt any conflict from the information in the half field that was ignored. The side of the brain that is not answering seems to switch off and not even see its side of the stimulus.

Of course the decision to respond with the left or right brain is not a conscious decision. Each hemisphere tries to solve the problem and the first one to feel strongly that it has a solution gives the answer. If both sides try to answer, the side that is more highly activated will inhibit the other one. Ideally, the hemisphere that dominates is also the one best qualified to answer, but this is not always so.

Jerre Levy recently reported another study[12] designed to determine on what basis the decision to activate one hemisphere or the other is made. Strong individual differences were found in the subjects. While some would use the hemisphere appropriate to the task, others would habitually use one hemisphere whether it was appropriate or not.

After one patient made a long sequence of left-hemisphere replies with his right hand pointing, the instructions and hand used for pointing were reversed to provide intentional "reinforcement" to the right hemisphere. After a large number of successful right-hemisphere replies, the instructions and hand used were changed back, but the right hemisphere continued to dominate the answers. It thus appears that the hemisphere that most strongly *thinks* it can do a task is the one that takes control.

After observing a similar split-brain experiment in progress in 1970 Oliver Zangwill made the following observation:[13]

> Under the special testing conditions designed by Levy, et al. (1972) to evoke "leading" activity in the minor hemisphere, it is possible to observe patients reacting under right-hemisphere control for appreciable intervals of time. In these circumstances, the subject may on occasion be observed to pass into a somewhat dreamy state, speaking little, if at all, and sometimes actually failing to respond when addressed by name. For some time thereafter, the patient may remain quiet or speak without modulation of the voice and with impoverished vocabulary. To an onlooker, it is difficult to avoid the impression that there has been some subtle change in the *quality* of the subject's consciousness, though it should be borne in mind that the *efficiency* of his performance is actually higher when the task is executed under right than under left hemisphere control.

This switching between the verbal and nonverbal mental state is a thing that normal people do all the time. The split-brain patients give us an opportunity to study it in its pure form and to relate it to hemispheres of the brain, but the basic mechanism is the same one that acts in normal brains. By understanding the aptitudes of the two hemispheres, we can hopefully learn to recognize when we are habitually using the wrong hemisphere. By intentionally allowing the appropriate hemisphere to prevail, we can reinforce its "confidence" in its own ability.

Language and the Right Brain

Though our right brain retains the more directly "parallel" way of thinking used by animals, it is clearly human and vastly superior to the mind of any other animal. The very first split-brain experiments demonstrated that the right brain can follow simple verbal instructions. It can read the word "pencil" and associate that word with a shape that feels like a pencil. When more complex definitions like "kitchen utensil," "container for liquids," "used for slicing," and "inserted in slot machines" are flashed to the right brain, the left hand is still able to retrieve, by touch, the corresponding object (the right hand, of course, cannot, since only the right hemisphere has knowledge of the object).[14]

The right brain can also make complex mental associations. For example, if a picture of a cigarette is flashed to the right brain, the subject's left hand can pick out an ashtray or box of matches from among nine other items not associated with cigarettes.[15]

One experimenter found that the right hemisphere can make four out of five kinds of mental associations.[16] For example, after feeling a spoon with the left hand, one patient could choose "fork," "soup," "silverware," and "cook" as related words. She could *not*, however, make the *abstract* associations such as relating a spoon to "nutrition." Abstract words and abstractions are strictly verbal concepts and are therefore the province of the left hemisphere.

Though the right brain cannot *express* itself in words, it

understands a surprisingly large number of words. E. Zaidel, of the California Institute of Technology, recently developed an optical device[17] that blocks half of the visual field no matter how the subject moves his eyes. This makes it possible to give *standardized picture vocabulary tests* to each hemisphere of a split-brain patient *separately*. However, it is sometimes difficult to get the left brain to sit back and be quiet, since the left brain sees nothing but darkness while the right brain is being tested. To quote Zaidel:

> Thus one right hemisphere session, which was characteristically punctuated by claims that "I can't see a thing," "It's all dark," and by repeated denial of ability to respond, resulted in a new score of 80 on the Peabody [vocabulary] Test, while another session, which seemingly maximized right hemisphere independence (with repeated praise by the examiner for successful right hemisphere pointing and insistence on complete survey of the alternative choices before answering each item was attempted) yielded a raw score of 93 on the same test.

The lower score typifies what happens when the left brain seizes control and makes guesses because it feels that the right brain doesn't know what it is doing.

When Zaidel's apparatus was used to test the right-hemisphere vocabulary of two split-brain patients, the scores were surprisingly good for a "nonverbal" hemisphere.[18] The average right-brain "mental age" scores were 14.8 and 10.5 years, which was only slightly worse than their left-brain scores of 17.4 and 13.5 respectively. Since there is some evidence of prior left-brain damage, these scores may not be typical. They do show, however, that at least some people have significant language comprehension in both hemispheres.

Though both right brains were fairly good at recognizing single words, their performance fell to *below the five-year-old level* on another test called the Token test. While the picture vocabulary tests involve simply pointing to one of four pictures representing a single dictated word, the Token test[19] uses a long sentence as the stimulus. A typical Token test sentence is "Touch the small blue circle and the large green circle." It thus appears that the right brain is poorly equipped to analyze *long sequences*. This is consistent with other evidence that the right brain solves problems "in parallel" by analyzing the entire stimulus and coming up with an answer at one stroke. Words are simply recognized as sound or visual images, without phonetic analysis. The left brain, on the other hand, tends to analyze one step at a time and deduce an answer. The latter approach is obviously more effective for decoding the long phrases of the Token tests.

One of the surprising results of the Zaidel experiments is that the subjects' right brains understood verbs just as well as they did nouns. Earlier experiments by Gazzaniga and Sperry found that subjects were unable to follow printed commands like "laugh," "smile," "tap," or "hit" when they were flashed to the left visual field.[20] It is conceivable that the language ability of the right brain is a *passive* one whose function is primarily to make use of verbal information for clarifying the context of other sensations.

The errors made by the right brain in recognizing common words all involved confusions between *conceptually* similar words. For example, cup-spoon, table-chair, boy-girl, and dog-horse were confused. Usually such errors occurred in pairs; that is, if "dog" was confused with "horse," then "horse" was also confused with "dog."[21] These errors are further evidence of the *concept* orientation of the right brain.

Another interesting thing about the kind of errors made on the picture vocabulary tests is that they did not seem to depend upon how commonly used the word was. The difference between the left- and right-hemisphere scores remained about the same for obscure words as it did for very common words. This is a very significant finding because it shows that the right brain's vocabulary is not just something left over from childhood. If it were, the right scores would be much larger for the simple words learned in childhood than for less often used words. It appears that the vocabulary of the right brain continues to grow in adulthood.

Language Expression by the Right Brain

The ability to understand words and simple sentences does not necessarily imply that the right brain can *create* sentences. Expressive language is a much more complex process in that words must be assembled into a meaningful order. While no conflict is created by having both hemispheres *understand* speech simultaneously, it is obviously impractical for both to try to express themselves at the same time.

The left brain's monopoly on expressive language is so strong that most of the split-brain patients are unable to demonstrate any right-brain expressive language. Part of the problem is that it is very difficult to get the left brain to yield control of the vocal apparatus or even the muscles of the left arm when left-handed writing is attempted. Levy, Nebes, and Sperry[22] had some success with one subject by giving him two or three plastic letters, hidden from view, and asking him to arrange them with his left hand into a word. Since the names of the letters had to be determined by feeling them with the left hand, the left brain was not aware of their identity. The patient was able to spell "if," "can," "boy," "pet," "by," and "so" in this way. Verbally he could not say what the words were, even after the letters were arranged. The person was also able to write words like the above with his left hand after feeling them with the left hand. In a few cases he was able to verbalize the words only after having written them with his left hand.

It was later found that if the examiner moved the subject's passive left hand through the motions of writing the words, he could also identify them. In the five years since his operation, the patient probably has developed his left brain's natural ability to feel gross movements of the left hand and arm to the point where he can feel letters being written.

Similar problems were encountered when an attempt was made to have the patient write a word with his left hand after feeling the hidden object with his left hand. The first subject was consistently able to write only the first one or two letters of the word. Since writing a word is a long sequential operation, this may be another aspect of the right brain's limitation to "right now" parallel processing. In some cases the patient's left brain would become impatient, take control of the hand, and complete the word with an incorrect guess. The appearance of the letters and method of holding the pencil would abruptly change when the left brain took over.

Another subject was able to write twelve of thirty-nine simple words with his left hand after the words were flashed to the left visual field. This proved to be merely a case of copying the visual patterns, however, because he was unable to do the same thing when pictures were flashed instead of words.

The amount of expressive language in the right hemisphere varies tremendously among individuals. While most of the split-brain patients lack expressive right-brain language, one patient was recently found to have quite a bit.[23] This patient was actually able to answer questions flashed to the right hemisphere by arranging Scrabble letters with his left hand.

He was able to answer properly with his name, the day of the week, his girl friend's name, his hobby; and he even answered "good" when he was asked his mood. When asked his job preference, he spelled out *automobile race* *even though his left brain verbally claims that he wants to* *be a draftsman!* Could it be that we all have different goals in our right brain that go unexpressed because of the left brain's monopoly on language?

One exception to the left-brain monopoly on verbal expression may be cursing and other short emotional exclamations. For example, in an experiment where the subjects identified smells presented to one nostril, some strong smells presented to the right hemisphere produced verbal exclamations like "ugh," "yuk," or "phew."[24] In spite of this verbalization the subject was still unable to identify the smell verbally, but could choose a related shape with the left hand. The right hemisphere is therefore capable of controlling speech but is normally prevented from doing so by strong competition from the left.

As we shall see in the next chapter, the right brain's speaking ability is still tragically inadequate even when it is completely free of competition from the left.

Chapter 10

THE DAMAGED BRAIN

Each year in the United States alone there are some 300,000 victims of brain damage due to stroke. Strokes generally happen to people who are over forty and therefore fully developed mentally. Strokes damage the brain by oxygen starvation, when a blood vessel feeding the brain either bursts or gets clogged.* Larger strokes give an unmistakable signal as to which hemisphere is affected by complete or partial paralysis of one side of the body. A stroke in the right hemisphere causes numbness or paralysis on the left side of the body but leaves the patient's language abilities intact. These patients are lucky because they can get along reasonably well in our left-brained society. Their most serious handicaps on a daily basis are a tendency to get lost, poor memory for nonverbal things, and a certain emotional flatness.

Strokes that numb or paralyze the right side of the body

* Clogging is generally caused by fat deposits or a blood clot lodged in an artery. When brain cells are deprived of blood circulation for more than a few minutes, they are damaged irreparably. Many strokes affect such a tiny area of the brain that their effects go unnoticed.

are much more serious. Since they result from left-hemisphere damage, they generally cause partial or complete loss of normal speech (called aphasia). Since the brain tissue does not heal, only limited improvement due to brain reorganization is possible. The tragedy of this type of stroke is that the patient is fully conscious, and even understands much of what is being said, yet he is unable to verbalize his thoughts.

This loss of speech is often not complete, since only a part of the left hemisphere is usually destroyed. Two classic types of aphasia have been identified and related to damage to specific parts of the left brain: Broca's aphasia results from damage to an area that apparently initiates the production of spoken and written language. A Broca's aphasic has difficulty in articulating speech but not in understanding it. His speech is halting and completely lacking in grammatical niceties. Often sentences sound much like a telegram with all but the most basic words omitted. The Broca's aphasic is aware of his difficulty and is usually quite frustrated.

Wernicke described another type of aphasia in which the mechanisms of speech production are intact but the thought processes of the left brain are disordered. The result is a "word salad"—an impressive-sounding stream of double-talk, which makes little or no sense. In this case the patient's understanding of language is also impaired. The patient is not aware that he has any difficulty, nor is he frustrated, for his speech mechanisms are truly expressing his jumbled stream of verbal consciousness.

While the Wernicke's aphasia victim may have practically no understanding of spoken language, there is paradoxically one area where understanding remains intact: "Whole body" commands such as "stand up," "stand at attention," and "assume the position of a boxer" may be understood and obeyed with an understanding well above the patient's normal language comprehension ability.[1] It seems possible that this is the language ability of the intact right hemisphere in action. As we saw in the previous chapter, the right hemisphere's language ability is generally passive. However, control of the "whole body" positions is very well integrated in the brainstem, with inputs from both the left and the right hemispheres. Right-brain initiation of whole body movements in response to verbal commands not understood by the left brain thus seems possible.

Another paradox with Wernicke's aphasia victims is their ability to detect spelling errors in written material even though their own spelling is abominable. Their own spelling is, of course, controlled by their damaged left hemisphere. The still intact right brain, however, is able to recognize and point out spelling errors at a glance.

Effects of Right-Brain Damage

Since the patient with right-brain damage generally retains full use of language, his prospects for eventually resuming a fairly normal life are good. However, spatial disorientation immediately after the injury can be a serious problem. Hospitalized patients with right-brain damage commonly have difficulty finding their way to the bathroom and finding their way back to their beds. Even dressing can be difficult for these patients: The simple act of putting on a shirt can result in confusion with the shirt upside down or the arms in the wrong holes.[2] This spatial helplessness after a right-brain accident clearly demonstrates that the patient depended on his right hemisphere for help in these tasks before the stroke or accident.

Another serious problem that often occurs is the inability to recognize faces. Faces that have easily verbalized clues such as "black moustache" or "horn-rimmed glasses" are no problem, but the subtle distinctions that make most faces recognizable to normal people are simply not visible. Close friends and relatives (and sometimes even the patient's own face) are simply not recognizable.†

Though language ability is primarily a left-hemisphere function, right-brain damage can cause some problems with the more subtle aspects of language meaning. While *literal* meanings are readily understood, many right-damaged patients are unable to understand the more subtle, metaphorical aspects of language. For example, when asked to explain the proverb "Too many cooks spoil the broth," a right-hemisphere patient has no problem understanding the literal meaning, but he may be unable to understand that it could apply to other situations not involving food or cooks at all. To quote Howard Gardner in his book *The Shattered Mind:*[4]

> Indeed, the more one observes the right hemisphere patient's comprehension of questions (both literal and meta-

† In a 1962 study[3] of patients with brain injuries Hécaen found that of twenty-two patients unable to recognize faces, sixteen had predominantly right-brain damage, four had damage on both sides, and only two had damage on the left side (one of these was known to be left-handed).

phorical) and his own spontaneous language, the clearer his deficits in linguistic competence become. The patient's command of grammar and of sound structure seem unchanged, but the relationship between his capacity to express himself in language and his knowledge of the world is impaired. He resembles a kind of language machine, a talking computer that decodes literally what is said, and gives the most immediate (but not necessarily the implicitly called for) response, a rote rejoinder insensitive to the ideas behind the questions, the intentions or implications of the questioner. And in his spontaneous speech, the patient again seems to neglect the emotional quality of the present situation or the extent of his impairment in favor of dispensing wisecracks—these, in turn, seem to reflect the operation of a "joke machine" rather than the holistic integration of feelings, situational cues, and interpersonal relations appropriate to a serious interview.

This emotional flatness is often accompanied by a flat, nonmusical tone of voice while speaking and an insensitivity to the meaning communicated by other people's tone of voice. Musical discrimination and sense of pitch are often lost after right-brain damage—a contributing factor. However, there is also a definite pattern of reduced emotional capability.

Researchers at the University of Florida[5] recently reported a study on the ability of brain-damaged patients to understand the emotional content of speech. They made a recording of four sentences spoken in each of four emotional moods: angry, happy, sad, and indifferent. This recording was played for twelve brain-damaged patients. Half of the patients had right-brain damage and half had left. Though five of the left-damaged patients had Broca's aphasia, they correctly identified the emotional meaning 64 per cent of the time. The patients with right-brain damage understood the *literal* meaning of the sentences perfectly but only identified the emotional meaning in 26 per cent of the trials. Since pure chance would give a score of 25 per cent, all six right-brain-damaged patients were apparently completely insensitive to the emotional tone of the sentences.

A systematic study of the emotional behavior of patients with left- and right-brain damage was published by Guido Gainotti in 1972.[6] A total of eighty left- and eighty right-damaged patients were examined. The results clearly showed that the undamaged right brain is more inclined to have strong emotional reactions, particularly negative ones. Catastrophic reactions, such as crying, swearing, and refusal to cooperate, occurred primarily in patients with left-brain damage (intact right hemisphere). Indifference reactions, joking, and denial or minimization of illness tended to accompany right-brain damage (intact left hemisphere). The catastrophic reactions of the left-damaged patients are not surprising when one considers the frustration of the intact right brain due to difficulties in language expression.

The indifference reactions of the right-damaged patients, on the other hand, show a real lack of normal emotional response. These patients are hospitalized for brain damage and in many cases have paralysis of one side of their body and serious spatial disorientation. Indifference and joking under those circumstances show a lack of emotional response that is characteristic of the left brain alone.

The reason for the different degrees of emotional depth of the two hemispheres may be found in their different basic organizations. The right brain reacts to sensory information in a more primitive and direct way, so the feelings retain their immediateness and power. In the left brain the sensory inputs tend to be interpreted in words and thus lose much of their emotional value. The dichotomy is thus between a cold intellectual approach and a "gut level" approach.

The Language of the Corpus Callosum

In a normal person's brain the two hemispheres are continually exchanging information by means of the corpus callosum and other neural connections between the hemispheres. When we look straight ahead and verbally describe what we see, the verbal description originates in our left brain. Since only the right side of our visual field is connected to the left brain (see Figure 2, page 8), anything we describe on the left has been passed over the corpus callosum from our right hemisphere.

Since the neural fibers of the corpus callosum seem to interconnect equivalent points in the higher associational levels of the two hemispheres,[7] they clearly do *not* deal in raw sensory information. The information passed by the corpus callosum appears to be already processed, higher-level information. One of the best sources of insight in this matter is brain damage cases in which *part* of the corpus callosum is damaged.

In 1892 a French neurologist, Joseph Jules Déjerine, described a fascinating case[8] of "word blindness." His patient was a successful businessman in his sixties who awoke one morning to find that he could no longer read. Yet *he could still see everything except words and letters* without a problem. While he couldn't *identify* letters, he could see them as shapes and even make exact copies of them. He could not, however, copy block letters in his own handwriting because that would require identifying them as letters.

When the man died, Déjerine found that a stroke had destroyed the visual cortex of his left brain and rear portion of his corpus callosum. With the visual cortex destroyed, the left brain was essentially blind. The man's verbal consciousness could still "see" because visual information from his right brain's normal vision was passed over the intact portion of his corpus callosum to his left brain. The information that was passed, however, was *obviously not raw visual information* because the man could see things, but not words. The right brain apparently *processes* what it sees and passes the *results*, rather than raw visual information, to the left brain. If raw visual data were passed over the corpus callosum, damage to part of it would cause blindness in part of the visual field, rather than blindness to specific *kinds* of things. Apparently different kinds of already classified information are passed between the hemispheres by different parts of the corpus callosum.

This patient's selective blindness offers a clue to how we perceive what we see. For example, though he could not read letters and words, he could recognize certain familiar trademarks and logos. Though the letters "R" and "F" by themselves were not recognized, the patient immediately said "République Française" when shown the French emblem "RF." He could likewise instantly recognize the newspaper *Le Matin* by its distinctive masthead. Advertising people have the right idea when they stress recognition of a simple trademark. Such symbols are recognized as objects or faces would be—by the right brain. Just as we recognize a face in a crowd instantly, the right brain can recognize a trademark or logo in a crowd of products—without even reading it. The impulsive decision to buy a certain item may thus result from the unconscious recognition of it by the right brain.

While the previous case involved destruction of the rear portion of the corpus callosum, let's look at another case in which the front portion was destroyed. This case[9] was discovered in 1962 by Edith Kaplin and Norman Geschwind, of Boston Veterans Hospital. While this patient had no problem reading words flashed to either side of his field of vision, he was unable to transfer touch or movement commands between the hemispheres. When he felt objects with his left hand with his eyes closed, he was completely unable to *name* them even though his left hand was able to use them properly. For example, while holding a pair of scissors properly and making cutting motions with them, he said, "I'd use that to light a cigarette with."

Dictated sentences were correctly written with the right hand, but the left hand wrote only meaningless gibberish. When the patient saw the incorrect productions of his left hand, he was astonished. Block letters could be copied in handwriting by the right hand, but the left hand could only copy them exactly, as one would copy meaningless pictures.

In summary Dr. Geschwind concluded that the patient "appears to behave as if there were two nearly isolated half-brains, functioning almost independently."

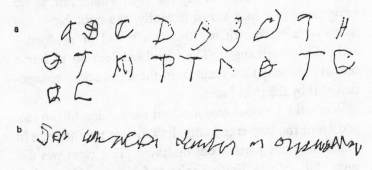

14. *Samples of handwriting with the left hand by Geschwind's patient with accidental disconnection. (a) is the alphabet while (b) is an attempt to write "To come early was impossible" from dictation. The same things were written correctly by the right hand.*

The patient's left-handed writing shows many of the *detailed features* of normal left-handed writing. Yet the *programming* of these features was being done incorrectly by the disconnected right hemisphere. Again it appears that it is *higher level commands*, rather than detailed commands for individual muscle movements, that are sent over the corpus callosum. A "T," for example, would require a left-hemisphere command for each of its two elements, but the detailed muscle movements would be done automatically by learned motor skill "subroutines" in the motor area of the hemisphere opposite the hand doing the writing.

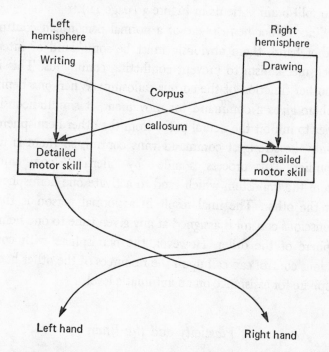

15. *Schematic diagram of the brain hemispheres. Motor skills for detailed movement of each hand reside in the hemisphere on the opposite side of the body. These detailed movements can be programmed by either hemisphere. Writing with either hand is programmed by the left brain while drawing is programmed by the right brain.*

When a normal person writes with either hand, the high-level commands come from the left hemisphere. When we draw with either hand, the commands come from the right hemisphere. The motor skill for a particular hand stays the same no matter which hemisphere does the programming. This can clearly be seen in the drawings of the split-brain patients in Figure 3 (page 11).[10]

Since either hemisphere of a normal person can control either hand, there obviously must be some kind of interlock mechanism to prevent conflicting commands. This is another function of the corpus callosum: When one hemisphere gives a command for movement, it simultaneously tries to inhibit the neural paths from the other hemisphere. Only the strongest command wins control, so there is no conflict. This process is aided by "alerting" commands from the brainstem which tend to activate one hemisphere or the other. The final result in a normal person is that conscious control is assigned at any given time to one hemisphere or the other. However, the hemisphere with conscious control can call upon the resources of the other hemisphere for assistance on an automatic level.

Plasticity and the Brain

Unlike the rest of the body, damaged brain cells never heal. However, the brain does recover to some degree by a process similar to learning. For example, damage to one side of the brain often causes paralysis of the limbs on the opposite side. Rehabilitation of gross movement is possible because there are already some incomplete and poorly developed nerve connections from the hemisphere on the same side as the paralysis (see Appendix II). Physical therapy after the injury effectively "educates" these nerve connections to a higher level making significant improved muscle control possible.

One spectacular case has been reported[11] which demonstrates the tremendous plasticity of the infant brain. Despite complete removal of the *left* hemisphere at the age of five and a half years, this patient was found to have a *verbal IQ of 126*, twenty-one years after his operation. His performance IQ score was 102, indicating lower, but still average ability with nonverbal thinking. He has a job as a traffic controller and is simultaneously completing his senior year at a prominent midwestern university. While this is certainly a rare case, it does demonstrate that either hemisphere is physically capable of developing superior language ability.

The real commitment of the left brain to language seems to begin at about the age of five. Prior to this age, injuries to either side of the brain will not usually cause permanent loss of language ability.

As the brain matures and higher language abilities develop, the tendency for permanent language impairment with left-brain injury and no language impairment with right injury increases. A fully mature adult with injury to the speech areas of the left brain has little hope of recovering normal speech.‡

Once the *organization* of the brain is committed, it is impossible to accomplish a total reorganization.[12] The mature patient is thus limited to retraining and improvement

‡ A large-scale study by Luria on the war wounded found that 97.2 per cent of all patients with wounds in the primary speech area of the left hemisphere were aphasic on first examination. A follow-up examination found that 93.3 per cent were still aphasic (though generally to a lesser degree).

within the framework of his existing brain organization, while the child's brain can actually reorganize to work around damage.[13]

Surgical Removal of Half of the Brain

In 1929 W. E. Dandy, of Johns Hopkins Hospital, reported that a dramatic operation, called a hemispherectomy, had been performed on five patients in which the *entire* right hemisphere of the brain was removed. Apart from relieving the patients' symptoms, Dandy reported that removal of the right hemisphere had no discernible effects on the language, general intelligence, or personality of the patients. Time has proven Dandy's reports to be somewhat overenthusiastic, but the operation continues to be used on children and on adults who have a hopelessly spreading brain tumor.

The remarkable thing about hemispherectomy is that the patient's IQ and other mental abilities are often *improved* by the operation. One unusually successful operation on a nineteen-year-old man[14] raised his IQ scores from 101 verbal and 63 performance before the operation to 121 verbal and 91 performance fifteen years after. Though he had only a left hemisphere, he earned a university diploma and works successfully in a government administrative job.

The reason mental performance is often improved after these operations is that in the competition for control, the damaged hemisphere is often able to inhibit the healthy one and prevail with wrong results. With the damaged hemisphere removed, the healthy one is free to take over all tasks.[15]

The Right Brain's Contribution to Personality

In spite of the fact that right hemispherectomy patients have continued normal verbal IQ, language, and math ability, very few of them ever return to a normal life and job. Their left hand is typically paralyzed except for gross movements, and walking, if learned at all, is awkward due to lack of subtle muscle control on the left. These movement problems by themselves, however, are not serious enough to explain the patient's continued disability. Even their lack of spatial ability is not serious enough to prevent their returning to useful lives. The real problem is that there is a subtle pattern of mental and personality defects that reflect the right brain's contribution to what we call a normal person. One summary of ten adult hemispherectomy cases described this pattern as follows:[16]

> With one exception . . . the individuals operated on for brain tumor suffered a loss in terms of personality values. They became dependent, regressive and ineffective people. Systematic psychological tests demonstrate that in most of these subjects intellect *per se* is not the outstanding deficit, for vocabulary and verbalization appear to suffer the least and memory and more complex integrations involving insight, emotional control, initiative, constructive ideation, and imagination that hemispherectomy takes its toll.

Another report on four adult hemispherectomies stated:[17]

> . . . we observed a loss of interpersonal relationships, a flattened affect, and generalized blunting of personality. . . .

As an example of the loss of affect, this same doctor described his interview with one of the patients six weeks after his operation:

"Al, how do you feel?"

"With my hands" was the reply without any change in voice tone or facial expression.

Also, a report on a case ten years after right hemispherectomy notes:[18]

> . . . the relative freedom from severe physical handicap and gross mental defect after removal of almost half the cerebrum was striking. . . . Penfield (1934) stated that the defect produced by a frontal lobectomy is a lack of capacity for planned administration and the loss of power of initiative. Study of our cases has indicated that this is the most accurate description of the mental defect produced by removal of the right cerebral hemisphere. . . .

Since these personality defects appear after removal of the right hemisphere in people who have reached adulthood normally, we can conclude that the right brain makes an important contribution to what we call a normal personality.

Removal of the Left Brain

Because of the importance of vital language capabilities, removal of an adult's left hemisphere is much less common than removal of the right. There have been a few cases reported, however, where speech is sacrificed to keep the patient alive and the entire left hemisphere is removed. The patient typically loses all language except for the ability to *curse*. For example, in 1966 Aaron Smith reported in detail the case of a forty-seven-year-old man called E.C.[19] Immediately after the operation, E.C. was unable to answer questions with meaningful speech, but he was able to clearly articulate "expletives and short emotional phrases" such as "goddammit!" He could not repeat single words on command or communicate in propositional speech until months later when occasional sentences could be produced. While removal of the right hemisphere causes flat, unemotional speech, removal of this patient's left brain left nothing but the most emotional of speech. Even more important, the personality deficits of the right-hemispherectomy patients were not a problem in this case. To quote the original report:

> Loss of personality values or bizarre behaviour reported after similar cases with right hemispherectomy (Gardner et al., 1955), however, was not observed in E.C. Affective reactions and general behaviour I have observed before and after hemispherectomy were appropriate, and consistent with his wife's report of no noticeable change in emotional responses or in a basically well-balanced personality.

Five months after the operation E.C.'s scores on picture completion, block design, picture arrangement, and object assembly test were only slightly lower than they were before the operation. Even his Wechsler performance IQ was *virtually the same* as it was before the operation. In fact his score of 110 puts him in the top 25 per cent of the general population in nonverbal reasoning ability. The patient's verbal IQ, of course, dropped to zero after the operation, though it was an above-average 115 before the operation.

For the first five months after the operation E.C. was easily fatigued and therefore hard to test. Hence it is difficult to tell how much of his improvement results from physical recovery from the operation and how much represents learning by his intact right brain. For example, forty-nine days after the operation he was able to pick up correct numbers of blocks from one to five on verbal command but could not select correct answers to simple addition problems. After five months, he could select correct answers to simple addition, subtraction, multiplication, and division problems. His ability to understand spoken language likewise improved. After six months, he was able to correctly select one of four pictures representing a dictated word in 85 out of 112 trials (the Peabody picture vocabulary test). Some examples of correctly understood words were "precipitation," "hieroglyph," "orate," "cascade," and "illumination."

In spite of his sizable comprehension vocabulary, E.C. continued to be unable to write or speak language. The organization of the right brain seems to be incompatible with expressive language. One dramatic exception was his ability to sing entire familiar songs. For example, E.C. could sing "My Country, 'Tis of Thee," "Home on the Range," and various church hymns "with little hesitation and few errors of articulation."[20] As time went by, E.C. was increasingly able to answer questions correctly with simple phrases. He moved about the hospital independently in his wheel chair, used the self-service elevator, told time, and kept appointments in the hospital without being reminded. He was permitted to go home on weekends after the third month, and his "libidinal drives" were reported to be normal. In the twentieth month after the operation E.C.'s test performance fell off sharply. As is often the case, his brain tumor reappeared in the remaining hemisphere and eventually caused his death.

Only two other cases of left hemispherectomy after infancy have survived long enough for proper study. These patients were only ten and fourteen years old at the time of their operation.[21] In both cases simple spoken language was well understood, but expressive language was very limited.

The ten-year-old's language ability was studied extensively two years later. She could sing complete songs correctly, but could speak only single words or short phrases. Though she could rapidly recite the alphabet correctly, she could only write the first few letters accurately. It appears that the right brain can store lengthy *automatic sequences* of speech but cannot *create* a long sequence of words. The problem seems to be related to an inability to relate things that are separated in time by more than a few seconds. Verbal understanding is also limited to fairly short sentences. This is not surprising, since the right brain seems to deal with things "at one stroke" rather than as a logical sequence.

In spite of the loss of most expressive language, personality and emotion largely remain without the help of the left hemisphere. To quote from the little girl's case history:

> . . . personality characteristics such as humour, boredom, love, and frustration are readily exhibited by the right hemisphere in a pattern reported by the parents to be substantially the same as before surgery.

Switching Off One Hemisphere
with Shock Treatment

One of the old reliable treatments for mental illness is shock therapy. Basically shock therapy works on the same principle as fixing your television set by banging on it. However, since it sometimes actually works when other methods fail, it is still in use today. A shock treatment is an artificially induced grand mal epileptic seizure. Electrodes are placed on the scalp and pulsed with electricity, which causes a spreading "electrical storm" in the brain. After strong muscular convulsions, the patient is left quivering and unconscious. Breathing must be maintained with a respirator for the first few minutes. Approximately six minutes after shock is applied the patient begins to remember his name, and within about ten minutes he can remember his age and where he is now. Generally the patient's brain activity and memory are greatly reduced for days, and in fact his brain waves (measured on an EEG) are still abnormal several weeks after the treatment.[22] Since the patient must essentially reorganize his thoughts after each shock treatment, his condition often improves after a sequence of treatments.

In 1958 it was discovered[23] that by shocking *only one side of the brain* the same benefit could be obtained with much less confusion and trauma to the patient. For *only the side given the shock is reduced to a state of stupor.* Instead of going into a complete stupor, the patient temporarily becomes a "left-brain person" or a "right-brain person," depending on which side didn't receive the shock treatment. It is somewhat like a temporary hemispherectomy. Within a few hours the shocked side recovers enough that the patient can again use both hemispheres. Vadim L. Deglin, one of Russia's leading neurophysiologists, has tested a large number of patients after unilateral shock treatments and has characterized the personality and abilities of what he calls the "left-hemisphere person" and the "right-hemisphere person."[24]

The "Left-Hemisphere Person"

After electroshock to the right hemisphere, the patient's left hemisphere is more active as a result of being freed of competition from the right. The patient becomes more talkative, sometimes to an excessive degree. His vocabulary becomes richer and more varied and his answers are more extensive and detailed. At the same time his intonation is less expressive; it is monotonous, colorless, and dull. His voice itself acquires a kind of nasal twang, or becomes unnatural, as though the patient were barking.[25]

A similar defect is observed in the patient's sensitivity to tone of voice: The left hemisphere by itself is unable to detect things such as anger, playfulness, or enthusiasm as communicated by intonation of the voice. Even the difference between a male and female voice is often undetectable without the help of the right brain. When tape recordings of natural sounds such as coughing, laughter, snoring, and breaking surf are played, the patient either cannot identify them or takes a long time to identify them.

Often the left hemisphere will attempt to classify the

sound rather than identify it. For example, instead of saying, "That's a dog barking," he will say, "That's an animal." Often the classification is wrong, but the very effort to classify is symptomatic of the left-hemisphere approach.

Another defect that occurs is the inability to sing or recognize well-known tunes. When asked to hum along with music, the patient will generally hum the wrong notes and eventually end up just tapping out the rhythm without the melody.

Visual perception is also impaired without the help of the right hemisphere. The patient will typically fail to notice missing details on uncomplicated pictures. For example, a pig with no tail or spectacles with no earpieces will go unnoticed. When asked to match pairs of simple geometric figures such as triangles, squares, etc., the patient is unable to do it if the figures are covered with confusing colored or striped sectors. This is the classic problem of not being able to "see the forest for the trees."

Though the patient can name the hospital, ward number, and other such verbal details, his visual recognition of his whereabouts is clearly impaired. He looks in bewilderment at the consulting room to which he has been a frequent visitor and says he has never been there before. While he can easily memorize and recite new verbal material, he is unable to memorize and identify shapes that are not easily given a verbal label.

Sometimes the "left-hemisphere person" is unable even to decide whether it is winter by simply looking out the window at snowdrifts and leafless trees. He may *deduce* that it is winter from the fact that the month is January, but the simple visual impression escapes him.

Generally the emotional outlook of these patients is easygoing and cheerful, even when they have a pattern of chronic depression or preoccupation with their illness in their normal state. It appears that the left brain is basically optimistic and cheerful even when the reality of their situation is depressing.

The "Right-Hemisphere Person"

When a patient receives shock therapy on the left side only, making him temporarily a "right-hemisphere person," his emotional outlook is transformed in the negative direction and he tends to become morose and pessimistic about his present situation and future prospects. He typically complains of not feeling well. His speech activity is greatly reduced. He is taciturn and, instead of answering questions in words, he prefers to respond by mime or gestures. It is difficult to converse with him, as he is inattentive to speech unless it is very loud. He often becomes silent after briefly answering one or two questions.

The speech of a "right-hemisphere person" shows a sharply diminished vocabulary and does not include words for abstract concepts. He has difficulty recalling names of objects, especially if they are infrequently used, but he is capable of explaining the purpose of any object or showing how it is used. His speech is made up of very simple sentences and often of isolated words. It is necessary to speak to him in very short and simplified sentences to be understood. His intonation and ability to recognize intonation in a voice is even better than in the normal state.

His hearing for nonverbal sounds is excellent and, in fact, he is more attentive to and better at perceiving natural sounds such as crashing surf than he would be with both halves of his brain working. He recognizes music immediately and tends to hum along without even being asked. Apparently the lack of competition from the left brain improves his performance on these tasks.

The task of matching geometric shapes covered with confusing colors and shapes is no problem to the "right-hemisphere person." Spotting missing details on pictures and memorizing complex shapes is likewise easy. While he can't say where he is or even give the date or year, he is visually oriented and is able to observe that he is in a hospital, without knowing which one. He recognizes the consulting room where he is sitting, although he cannot explain its purpose. He can also look out the window and determine what the season is, though he doesn't know the date.

If a "right-hemisphere person" is asked to arrange in pairs four cards with "V," "5," "10," and "X" on them, he will match them by visual appearance (5 with 10, V with X) rather than by abstract numeric value. A "left-hemisphere person" will do just the opposite and match numeric values (V with 5, 10 with X). A normal person would probably notice that there are two ways to match them and ask which strategy is desired.

Both the right and left hemispheres seem to have their own unique but overlapping archives of knowledge. While the "right-hemisphere person" doesn't "know" many of the words and abstract concepts that the "left-hemisphere person" does, he has his own unique store of visual memories, which the left hemisphere does not "know."

Putting Half of the Brain to Sleep

Another form of "temporary hemispherectomy," called the Wada test, was first introduced in 1949. It has been used on hundreds of patients prior to brain surgery to determine positively which hemisphere is dominant for speech. Basically the test[26] consists of injecting an anesthetic (sodium amytal) into the main artery feeding one hemisphere of the brain. The patient is asked to count and wiggle the fingers of both hands. When the drug takes effect, one hemisphere of the brain will be "asleep" as indicated by the opposite hand going limp. If the hemisphere injected is the one dominant for speech (usually left), the counting and all but the simplest speech will stop for about five minutes.

Sometimes the patient is still able to do confused counting and repeat some words, even though the left hemisphere is asleep. They can understand and follow verbal commands with their left hand indicating continued consciousness of the right brain. They can also sing with clearly recognizable pitch and rhythm.[27] Many patients verbalize songs and certain memorized jargonlike phrases with their right brain.

When the right brain is "put to sleep," normal speech continues (after a brief pause due to leakage of some anesthetic to the left brain). Singing becomes rhythmically correct but terribly off key or of a single note. About one third of all left-handed people seem to have their hemispheres organized the opposite of the normal way: They lose speech when the right brain is anesthetized and music when the left brain is "asleep."

As we have seen, left-brain-damaged patients who lose their powers of speech often recover partially but are left with aphasic speech. Aphasic speech has many characteristics similar to the known language limitations of the right brain. In four of six cases where the Wada procedure was tried on such patients,[28] speech stopped when the *right* brain was anesthetized but was unaffected by left injection. This indicates that the right brain had, in its limited way, taken over the speech functions formerly handled by the damaged left hemisphere. In many cases of left-brain damage, the aphasic speech is actually right-brain speech. The fact that an aphasic's first words are often emotional curses supports this finding.

One striking effect when either hemisphere is anesthetized is an extreme deviation of the eyes toward the anesthetized hemisphere. This is apparently an exaggeration of the normal "orientation response" in which the eyes look toward the side of the body attended by the active hemisphere. Anesthetizing one hemisphere grossly unbalances this competitive process.

A Left-Right Split Personality

In the normal brain, the left and right hemispheres seem to divide up tasks and cooperate enough that we appear to have a single personality. Certain types of behavior that don't fit this concept are explained as "moods" or as workings of the "subconscious mind." Occasionally, the normal mechanism for division of hemispheric function breaks down and a split personality develops.

While most split-personality cases can be explained in other ways,[29] a few are clearly cases of *separately functional left- and right-brain personalities*. The infant hemispherectomy cases have shown us that either hemisphere is capable of developing into a completely functional brain with its own speech and personality. In a few bizarre cases, two intact hemispheres seem to have developed so independently that *each* is capable of speech and each has its own personality. Depending upon which hemisphere is in control, the patient has one or the other distinct personalities. Each personality is accompanied by an opposite pattern of *hypersensitivity on one side of the body and numbness on the other!*

Two case histories of this type were described in detail in 1955.[30] One of the cases was a twenty-four-year old left-handed woman. The patient sometimes had a personality that was:

> . . . dependent, submissive, shy, self-effacing, affectionate, and obedient. . . . In a very timid way she expressed friendliness, sought affection, acceptance and approval from the personnel whom previously as Flossie she had reviled and abused. There was no trace left of any inappropriate word or expression, no manifestation of hostility to her surroundings and not the slightest reference to sex. In fact, any sex thought or word would induce in her ex-

treme fears of perdition, feelings of guilt and anxiety, depression, and shame.

Examination while this personality was active always showed a clear pattern of hypersensitivity on the right side and hyposensitivity on the left. Vision and hearing were unclear and far away on the left side but clear and close on the right. Sensitivity to touch and pain was high on the right side and low on the left. The left nostril was hypersensitive to smell while the right nostril was congested and insensitive to it. (The neural connections from the hemispheres to the nostrils are the only ones that do not cross. See Appendix II.) The right side of the patient's body showed a large pupil, hypersecretion of saliva, very strong sweating on palm and sole, and extremely strong abdominal reflexes. The left side of her body showed opposite symptoms: small pupil, no saliva or sweating, and no abdominal reflexes. The entire pattern indicated activation of the left hemisphere and inhibition of the right.

While this mental state would be stable for some time, an unexpected strong stimulus could trigger a complete reversal. The neurological symptoms would reverse, and simultaneously the patient would, in effect, become a different person. In this condition, she was:

> . . . impulsive, irresponsible, mischievous, and vindictive. . . . Full of rebellion against authority, and of hate toward the people around her, the patient in this phase was extremely aggressive, using abusive language and scaring other patients with lurid tales of state hospitals, sex relations, etc; on several occasions it was necessary to put her into the disturbed ward or even in seclusion.

In this state the patient was hypersensitive on the left side and numb on the right. In fact, all of the neurological symptoms of the other personality were reversed. It appears that the patient's right hemisphere was active and her left was inhibited.

When the patient was in one mental state, she was completely unaware of the existence, at another time, of the other personality. Apparently, the inactive hemisphere was so deeply inhibited that it had no memory of the times during which it was inactive.

The basis of this patient's problem seems to be a malfunction of the normal process in which one hemisphere becomes more active and inhibits the other. In a normal person the imbalance is not so drastic—the inhibited hemisphere remains alert enough to perceive what is happening and remain functional. This patient seemed to alternate effectively between *extremes of imbalance of activation resembling hemispherectomy*. Each hemisphere thus developed its own self-sufficient language capability and personality.

The Neglect Syndrome

In a normal person the two hemispheres have a harmonious working relationship based on specialization. As we have seen, verbal duties are handled by the left side and spatial tasks are done by the right. Another division of duties is a natural result of the crossed sensory connections to the hemispheres: Since the left brain sees and feels things to the right, it is in charge of responding to anything that happens on the right. The right brain likewise takes care of everything that happens on the left.

This left-right division of duties becomes very apparent immediately after damage to one side of the brain. One of the most common symptoms after right-brain damage is a complete neglect of everything happening on the left. A patient might shave only the right side of his face, forget to wear his left slipper, and put on his robe without putting his left arm in the sleeve.[31] Often patients will eat food only from the right side of their tray, and make drawings that omit the left side completely.

In most cases,[32] vision and sense of touch on the left are damaged, but the symptoms go far beyond anything that could be explained by this sensory loss. For example, if somebody speaks to the patient from the left, he may completely fail to respond. He will respond, however, if the sound comes from the right—even if the speaker is out of sight.[33] When a patient with neglect draws a picture and omits details on the left, the problem is not simply loss of vision on the left, because with small eye movements he can easily see the left side of the drawing. The problem seems rather to be a habit depending on the other hemisphere to attend to that side.

Often the patient will not raise his left arm when asked, even though in other circumstances he uses the arm without a problem. Sometimes the patient will deny that the arm belongs to him—even if the doctor holds it up where he can see it. In a sense the patient is right when he says that his left arm belongs to "someone else." The left brain is indeed used to having "someone else" control that arm:

The "someone else," of course, is the patient's now damaged right brain.

Generally the neglect syndrome is most serious immediately after an accident where the damage was abrupt. The most conspicuous aspects of neglect usually last no more than a few weeks.[34] The cure consists primarily of convincing the patient's left brain that it must stop rationalizing the inaction of his left side and start taking responsibility for things that were previously done by the damaged right brain.[35]

RIGHT AND LEFT BRAIN SPECIALIZATION

Left brain abilities	Right brain abilities
speech	
reading	understanding of metaphor
writing	
verbal memory consolidation	facial recognition
abstract categorizing	attending to left body and visual space
musical ability	spatial perception
fine manual sequences	ability to "find way"
	visual closure
	musical sense
seeing more than one thing at a time	form memory consolidation
left-right discrimination	
detail in drawings	*proper form* in drawings
Stanford-Binet Performance IQ (poor)	Stanford-Binet Performance IQ (poor)
Verbal IQ for Wechsler and Stanford-Binet Tests (worse)	Wechsler Performance IQ (poor)

Chapter 11

THE NORMAL BRAIN

Even though the two hemispheres of a normal person can exchange sensory information, this "secondhand" information is not as vivid as the direct information from the opposite side of the body. However, all of the left-right differences we saw in the split-brain patients can be demonstrated, although less dramatically, in normal people.

The reader himself can prove this by trying a simple experiment: *Stare at the nose* on each face and decide which face looks happier. By fixing the eyes on the nose, each half of the face is perceived by a different half of the brain. Though the left brain receives a conflicting input, the right-brain impression generally dominates since the right brain is more specialized for faces and nonverbal communications. Julian Jaynes,[1] the creator of this experiment, has shown it to almost a thousand people and found that 80 per cent of right-handed people say that the lower face is happier.[2] Responding to the left side of the face, of course, indicates that the right brain is dominating the decision. (The two faces are actually identical mirror images.)

16. *Stare at the nose on one face and then the other and decide which of the two faces is happier.*

If faces are flashed briefly to one side of vision or the other, most people will identify them more accurately on the left. If the same thing is done with words, the right visual field will be more accurate.[3] If we analyze the *kinds of errors* made in identifying words on one side or the other, we can see that the two hemispheres use distinctly different strategies. The errors made when the words are flashed on the left are more often words that *look* alike. This indicates that the right hemisphere tends to remember the word visually. Errors on words flashed to the right tend to be words that *sound* alike, reflecting the left brain's tendency to remember the word verbally.

Since the left brain thinks in words, it generally has an advantage in tasks where verbal mediation is useful. For example, if a sloped line is briefly flashed to either visual field and the subject is asked to identify it, the left brain (right field) will be more accurate in choosing the correct slope if the only possibilities are "vertical," "horizontal," and "slanted." If the number of possible slopes is increased so that it is no longer practical to remember what was seen verbally, the advantage switches to the right brain.[4] The left brain, therefore, has an advantage not only with verbal material but also with easily verbalized visual problems.

Serial and Parallel Thinking

We have already seen that the left brain tends to think in a serial one-step-at-a-time manner while the right brain uses a parallel approach. This difference in processing strategy has been demonstrated in normal people by measuring their reaction time to a task presented to the left or right visual field.[5] The task in this case was to recognize whether a given word was part of a set of words previously memorized. Subjects were asked to press a "yes" or "no" button as soon as they knew whether the word was one of those memorized.

When the word was flashed to the right visual field, reaction time got longer as the number of words in the memorized set was increased. This shows that the left brain was using the *serial* approach of comparing the word seen, one at a time, with each of the words memorized. Using this approach, of course, the more words there are to compare, the longer it takes to react.

When the word was flashed to the left visual field, the reaction time stayed the same no matter how many words were in the memorized set. The right brain thus appears to have been using a parallel approach in which the decision was made without examining each word separately. When the number of things to be remembered gets very large (as in face or picture recognition), this approach becomes indispensable.

Dichotic Listening Tests

One of the easiest tests for cerebral dominance on normal people is called a dichotic listening test. A good stereo tape recorder with stereo headphones is all that is needed to give the test. A special tape recording is used which presents conflicting words or sounds to the left and right ears. Though each ear has direct nerve connections to both halves of the brain, the connection to the hemisphere on the opposite side is a little stronger. When conflicting but equal strength audio signals are presented to the two ears, one ear or the other will tend to dominate depending on which hemisphere is better equipped to interpret the sound.[6]

For example, if *different words* are dictated simultaneously to the left and right ears, the subject will report primarily the words heard by the right ear. Though both signals are at the same volume, the *left* hemisphere hears the word presented to the right ear better. Since the left hemisphere is the speech specialist, its interpretation of what was heard will generally win out over the competing interpretation from the right hemisphere.

If, on the other hand, conflicting *nonspeech* sounds are presented simultaneously to both ears, the effect is reversed and the left-ear signal will tend to be reported. In this case the *right* hemisphere has a slight advantage because it specializes in nonspeech sounds.

Dichotic listening tests (in simplified form) have been given to children as young as three years old with basically the same results.[7] Below that age it is difficult to administer any test that requires the child to follow instructions. However, an ingenious method of dichotic testing of infants as young as three weeks old was recently reported by Anne Entus, of McGill University in Canada. Since the baby can't speak, his response is measured by recording how rapidly he *sucks on a special pressure sensing pacifier*. A change in the sound in his earphones starts him sucking more rapidly. The increase in sucking rate is thus effected by the amount and type of change in the sound that the baby hears.

When competing signals are presented to each ear and only *one* of the signals is changed, the baby will increase his sucking rate only if the change was in the ear that was dominating. The experiment was done with speech sounds such as "ma," "ba," "de," and with recorded musical instrument sounds. A total of forty-eight babies, averaging about three months old, were tested.

A strong right-ear (left brain) advantage for speech was found in 79 per cent of the infants. The music tests showed a left-ear (right brain) advantage in 71 per cent of the infants.[8]

Since these percentages are very close to those found in dichotic testing of older children and adults, it seems that the tendency to perceive speech with the left brain and music with the right is an inborn trait. At this stage of development the higher parts of the baby's brain and the corpus callosum are not even fully developed. In fact, speech and music as such really mean nothing to the baby; but the neural circuits are already showing a left-brain preference for speech sounds and a right-brain preference for music!

Left-Right Brain-Wave Studies

EEG (electroencephalogram) recordings are a powerful tool for observing the electrical activity of the brain. Metal contacts pasted on the scalp at various points measure the average electrical activity of the millions of neurons in the area of the contact. While this is a bit like testing a computer by placing a contact on the *outside* of the cabinet, there are certain observable gross patterns. For example, the "electrical storm" of an epileptic attack is clearly visible on an EEG.

When the normal brain is awake but idle, continuous waves of electrical activity called alpha waves dominate the EEG. The alpha rhythm seems to represent an "idling" state as it reaches a maximum when the eyes are closed and the mind is completely cleared of thought (as in meditation). When the eyes are opened or thinking occurs, the alpha rhythm is reduced in proportion to the degree of arousal.

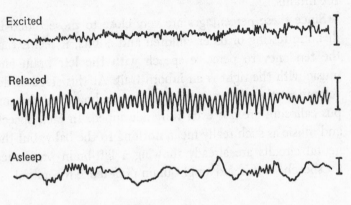

Excited

Relaxed

Asleep

17. Typical EEG recordings.

In 1972 Galin and Ornstein at the University of California Medical Center tried recording EEG signals from the left and right sides of the brain *separately* while the subject did verbal or spatial tasks. The result was an exciting confirmation that normal people tend to think with one side of the brain or the other. When the subject did a verbal task, the alpha rhythm was reduced on the left side but remained on the right. The right brain was thus continuing to idle, while the left brain worked on the problem! Spatial tasks gave the opposite result indicating right-brain processing.

The experiment[9] was performed on six normal subjects.

Each subject was given two different three-minute tasks designed specifically to engage the left or right brain. The left-brain task consisted of writing all the facts remembered from a newspaper article just read. The right-brain task consisted of constructing a pattern, just memorized, from sixteen multicolored blocks. Electrical signals from above the subjects' left and right ears were electronically filtered to measure only the *ratio* of right/left alpha signal power.

A ratio greater than one thus indicates left-hemisphere activation while less than one indicates that the right hemisphere is more active. The results are shown below:

	EEG Alpha R/L Ratio	
Subject №	Writing	Blocks
1a	1.63	0.37
1b (retest)	1.69	0.42
2	1.00	0.81
3	0.99	0.74
4	1.00	0.81
5	1.14	0.46
6	1.47	1.07
Geom. Mean	1.24	0.62

Though all of the subjects showed a change in left vs. right mental activity in the predicated direction, there was a tremendous variation between the individuals. Subject number two showed the least change (23 per cent). This probably indicates a tendency to use both hemispheres together for all types of tasks.

At the other extreme, subject number one showed such a strong (4:1) change in alpha ratio that the disbelieving experimenters tested him a second time. This high ratio indicates that he was essentially using one hemisphere *or* the other depending on which was best suited for the problem.

When we do something with one hemisphere strongly aroused and the other idling, the idle hemisphere is essentially "not paying attention." Thus one hemisphere may learn things while the other will not. This is why when we learn a right-brain task nonverbally, we find it hard to explain to others how to do it. Our verbal left brain *doesn't know* how to do it because it wasn't paying attention.

Eye Movement Studies

Since each hemisphere is primarily responsible for attending to the opposite side of the body, there is a reflex eye movement toward the opposite side whenever one side of the brain becomes attentive. Activation of the *left* hemisphere thus causes the eyes to orient *right*, since the right side of the body is under control of the left hemisphere.

This eye movement away from the activated side of the brain is an excellent indication of which hemisphere is being used. When a person is asked a question, his eyes will momentarily glance to the left or the right while he reflects on the answer. If the question is a verbal question, the eye movement will generally be to the right indicating left-hemisphere activation. If a question requiring spatial thought is asked, the eyes most often move to the left.

A typical eye movement experiment was recently reported by Raquel and Rubin Gur, of Stanford University.[10] They asked forty-nine male college students verbal and spatial questions while a hidden television camera recorded eye movements. The verbal questions required verbal explanations of proverbs such as "Rome was not built in a day" or "All that glitters is not gold." The spatial questions all required internal visualization. For example: "Visualize sitting in front of a typewriter. Where is the letter R relative to B?" or "Where is Chicago relative to Minneapolis?"

When the results were tabulated, it was found that the eyes moved to the right 64 per cent of the time after the verbal questions but only 31 per cent of the time after spatial questions.

Since there were over twice as many right-eye movements after verbal questions than after spatial questions, it appears that most of the students were using the appropriate side of their brain to solve the problems. This appropriateness almost totally disappeared, however, when the experiment was repeated with the examiner *facing* the subject instead of sitting behind him. Instead of moving the eyes in the direction that would indicate use of the hemisphere appropriate to the question type, each subject now moved his eyes in a consistent pattern, regardless of the question type.

It appears that the stress of face-to-face eye contact with the examiner made the subject rely on the hemisphere that he *habitually* depended on most—even if it was not the one appropriate to the question. Most of the subjects fell back on "old reliable" when there was real pressure. While only 16 per cent of the subjects moved their eyes in a habitual rather than appropriate direction when the examiner was out of sight, 71 per cent fell back on a habitual direction when the examiner faced them.[11]

Since mental performance certainly suffers when the appropriate hemisphere is not used, the majority of these students could greatly improve their performance under stress if they could just break this habit of favoring one hemisphere.

When the subjects were classified as "right-movers" "left-movers," and "bidirectionals" based on their habitual direction of eye movement (when facing the examiner), some very interesting personality correlations were found. This classification provides a good indication of which hemisphere is most easily activated and preferred regardless of the problem type. Each person, therefore, has a habitual "cognitive style" which partially determines his personality and aptitudes.

Generally right-movers have the typical left-brain tendency to major in sciences while the left-movers more often major in the humanities and social sciences. Bidirectionals fall somewhere in the middle, since they don't have a right- or left-brain habit. In an attempt to further characterize the personality types of the left-movers and right-movers, a psychological test designed to determine characteristic defense mechanisms was given to twenty-eight right-handed males who had been previously classified for their habitual direction of eye movement.[12]

The results of this experiment clearly showed opposite tendencies by the left-movers and right-movers. The right-movers had a strong tendency to handle their problems by externalizing them and "attacking a real or presumed external frustrating object." The left-movers, on the other hand, tended to handle problems in a more direct and internalized way by using reversal: Reversal involves repression or "responding in a positive or neutral fashion to the frustrating object."

Since repression is often associated with psychosomatic complaints such as headaches and ulcers, the subjects were also given a physical health questionnaire. The left-movers reported an average of 9.5 psychosomatic symptoms while right-movers reported only an average of 5.5.

Emotional Content and Eye Movement

Since the right brain is the specialist in emotional matters, we would expect emotional questions to evoke left-eye movements. Researchers at Harvard University reported an experiment[13] that not only confirmed this expectation but demonstrated how other factors can interact to activate one hemisphere or the other. They found that the spatial and the emotional content of questions are *additive* in their tendency to activate the right brain: While questions that had *either* spatial *or* emotional content would cause about one-third more right-brain responses, questions that contained *both* factors caused *twice as many* right-brain responses.

If we combine these results with our earlier findings about habitual cognitive style, it seems that *the activation of a hemisphere* by a question is the combined effect of several tendencies:

1. The tendency for the right brain to specialize in emotional matters.

2. The tendency for the right brain to specialize in nonverbal thinking and the left to specialize in verbal thinking.

3. The subject's own personal tendency to rely on the right or left brain, which is related to his personality and habitual approach to problems.

While the exact mechanism for this selective process of activating one hemisphere or the other is not known, it can be explained as the result of a kind of competition. If each half of the brain is separately conscious and "listening to the question," one of the hemispheres will have a "stronger feeling" that it can handle the problem.

Even though one consciousness or the other seems to dominate at any given time, it is obvious that each hemisphere in a normal person is able to call upon the resources of the other half. For example, we can easily describe verbally what we see in our left visual field or what we feel with our left hand. This information is, of course, coming from the right brain by way of the corpus callosum. Our verbal consciousness can even call upon such right-brain abilities as facial recognition without having to yield conscious control to the right.

In a normal brain it appears that the competitive mechanism that puts one hemisphere or the other in conscious control does not necessarily exclude the other hemisphere from helping on an automatic level.[14] This selection mechanism thus prevents conflicts from occurring but still allows nonoverlapping functions in the other half of the brain to be used. For example, the left brain can use the motor skills of the right brain to do left-handed writing.

The split-brain patients lose this ability to a large degree. For instance, when a split-brain patient was asked to tap both fingers while talking, his right hand stopped tapping as he groped for a verbal response.[15] A normal person has no such problem because his right hemisphere can keep the tapping going while the left is busy thinking. Though a normal person can have only one train of *conscious* thought at a time, he can easily perform other automatic functions while thinking. Talking and driving a car, for example, are compatible as long as the driving situation is routine.

The marvelous and complex interactions of the human mind may never be completely understood. Though the view we have developed is undoubtedly oversimplified, it is an important first step. The human mind has at last discovered the secret of its own duality. The magical synergy of logic and intuition, which until now has been left to chance, can finally be understood and encouraged.

Appendix I

BRAIN DAMAGE SYMPTOMS VS. SIDE OF DAMAGE

The table that follows was borrowed from an excellent paper by Hécaen and Sauguet (1971). While the original paper was concerned mainly with left-handedness, the tabulation of symptoms vs. side of damage for 560 patients is extremely interesting as a guide to which hemisphere is primarily responsible for each kind of ability. The numbers in the "p" column indicate the probability that the observed left-right distribution could happen by chance ("ns" means statistically not significant). The number of patients included in the data was:

293 right-handers with left-brain damage (lesions)
194 right-handers with right-brain damage
47 left-handers with left-brain damage
26 left-handers with right-brain damage

The meaning of most of the medical terms used can be found in the glossary.

BRAIN DAMAGE SYMPTOMS VS SIDE OF DAMAGE

	Right-handers			Left-handers		
	Left-sided lesions %	Right-sided lesions %	p	Left-sided lesions %	Right-sided lesions %	p
Disturbances of oral language						
Articulatory disorders	13	0	.0005	18	4	ns
Naming disorders	38	0	.0005	31	12	ns
Comprehension	33	0	.0005	11	8	ns
Paraphasias	13	0	.0005	10	12	ns
Disturbances of reading						
Letters	10	0	.0005	13	4	ns
Words	16	0	.0005	14	8	ns
Digits	8	0	.0005	9	8	ns
Numbers 2-3 digits	16	3	.0005	21	8	ns
Numbers > 3 digits	28	6	.0005	26	12	ns
Simple commands	23	1	.0005	22	8	ns
Complex commands	33	1	.0005	31	8	.10
Textual material	38	16	.0005	58	23	.025
"Spatial" dyslexia	1	22	.0005	7	31	.01
Disturbances of writing						
Letters-words	29	2	.0005	18	12	ns
Sentences	44	4	.0005	44	16	.05
Story	44	4	.0005	39	14	ns
Copy	20	3	.0005	26	10	ns
Spelling	30	2	.0005	18	5	ns
Digits	12	0	.0005	7	4	ns
Numbers	30	1	.0005	29	8	.10
"Spatial" dysgraphia	4	25	.0005	9	31	.01
Disturbances of calculation						
Anarithmetia	53	18	.0005	56	15	.01
Mental calculation	54	5	.0005	38	10	ns
Arithmetic signs	23	6	.01	21	10	ns
Recognition of position of digits within a number	44	18	.0005	25	29	ns
"Spatial" dyscalculia	0	19	.0005	2	27	ns
Counting	3	25	.0005	4	23	ns

	Right-handers			Left-handers		
	Left-sided lesions %	Right-sided lesions %	p	Left-sided lesions %	Right-sided lesions %	p
Apraxias						
Ideatory apraxia	1	0	ns	2	0	ns
Ideomotor apraxia	10	0	.0005	2	0	ns
Constructional apraxia	25	45	.0005	26	59	.005
Apraxia for dressing	0	16	.0005	9	9	ns
Disturbances of somatognosis						
Right-left orientation						
On the patient	2	0	ns	2	0	ns
On the observer	10	5	.10	12	17	ns
Finger gnosis						
Naming	19	1	.0005	13	8	ns
Verbal designation	14	1	.0005	3	9	ns
Non-verbal designation	5	1	.05	0	8	ns
Autotopognosis	3	0	.05	2	4	ns
Hemiasomatognosia	0	9	.0005	4	13	ns
Disturbances of visual recognition						
I - Spatial data						
Spatial disorientation	2	11	.0005	0	17	ns
Unilateral spatial agnosia	0	31	.0005	5	32	.001
Topographic notions	8	16	.01	9	9	ns
Depth appreciation	2	6	.01	2	9	ns
Metamorphopsias	6	10	.05	11	12	ns
Subjective visual coordinates	21	41	.0005	20	38	.10
II - Recognition of images and colors						
Recognition of complex figurative picture	1	4	.05	0	0	ns
Recognition of designs of well-known symbols	4	7	.05	4	5	ns
Naming of colors	15	0	.0005	16	0	ns
Classification of colors	16	4	.0005	12	0	ns
Color evocation	5	0	.0005	3	0	ns
Color designation	5	0	.005	9	0	ns

NERVE CONNECTIONS TO BRAIN HEMISPHERES

Function	Left Brain (verbal)	Right Brain (nonverbal)
Vision	Right half of visual field, both eyes	Left half of visual field, both eyes
Smell	Left nostril	Right nostril
Hearing	Both ears (slightly stronger to right)	Both ears (slightly stronger to left)
Touch	Right side, gross sensations on left, both sides of head	Left side, gross sensations on right, both sides of head
Facial muscles	Both sides (stronger to right)	Both sides (stronger to left)
Hands	Right side, gross movements only on left	Left side, gross movements only on right
Body muscles	Right side, some movement on left	Left side, some movement on right

GLOSSARY

While I have avoided the use of technical terms in this book, this glossary is included for those who would like to read further the medical journals referenced.

A- An "a" preceding Latin medical terms indicates a loss or malfunction.

AFFECT Emotional response, feeling.

AGNOSIA Inability to recognize objects.

ALEXIA Inability to read.

ALPHA WAVES Regular electrical waves in the brain at five to ten cycles per second. The amplitude of alpha waves in a person is reduced in proportion to their arousal.

AMNESIA Loss of memory.

ANARITHMETIA Inability or difficulty with calculation.

ANOMIA Inability to name objects, although they are subjectively perceived.

ANTERIOR Toward the front.

APHASIA Inability or difficulty in speaking and writing.

APRAXIA   Inability to execute purposeful movements.

AUTOTOPAGNOSIA   Inability to recognize any part of the body.

BLOCK DESIGN   A test of spatial-constructional ability (right brain) in which blocks with pattern segments painted on them are assembled to duplicate a more complicated pattern.

BRAINSTEM   The lower portion of the brain, including the medulla and pons.

BROCA'S AREA   The lower middle portion of the left hemisphere. Crucial to the production of speech.

CEREBELLUM   A spherical mass nestled under the rear of the cerebral cortex and attached to the spinal cord. It controls balance of the body and automatic motor sequences like walking. (See Figure 1, page 5.)

CEREBRAL CORTEX   The two hemispheres which constitute the top 80 per cent of the brain in man. (See Figure 1, page 5.)

CEREBRUM   Another name for cerebral cortex.

CLOSURE   Elimination of gaps in the information required to solve a problem.

COMMISSURES   The neural connections between the left and right hemispheres of the cerebral cortex. (See Figure 1, page 5.)

COMMISSUROTOMY   An operation in which all or most of the connections between the left and right hemispheres are cut.

CONFABULATION   Making up stories—often to explain disabilities that the patient denies.

CONSTRUCTIONAL   Relating to the ability to put things together such as blocks in a block test or picture elements in a drawing.

CONTRALATERAL   On the opposite side of the body.

CONVERGENT THINKING   The logical thinking process strives toward order and logical consistency. The opposite of divergent thinking.

CORPUS CALLOSUM   A long band of nerves connecting the left and right hemispheres. (See Figure 1, page 5.)

CORRELATION COEFFICIENT   The degree of interrelationship between two sets of data. A correlation coefficient of 1 means that they are identical, while 0 indicates no relationship. A negative coefficient means that the data varies oppositely.

CORTEX   Cerebral cortex.

CRANIOTOMY   Surgical opening of the skull prior to brain surgery.

DEXTRAL   Right-handed, opposite of sinistral.

DIVERGENT THINKING   The fluent search for new ideas. Opposite of convergent thinking.

DYSLEXIA   Difficulty with reading.

EEG   Electroencephalograph. A recording of faint electrical signals on the scalp which result from the electrical activity of the brain.

EMBEDDED FIGURES TEST   Test to determine how well a subject can find hidden figures in a complex drawing; e.g., a face in a tree. A measure of field dependence.

ENGRAM   A memory record in the brain.

EPILEPSY   A disorder in which an injured spot in the brain produces an electrical discharge which spreads through the brain. A major seizure can cause massive muscle contractions and unconsciousness while a minor one is hardly noticeable.

FIELD DEPENDENCE Inability to separate a stimulus from its surrounding context. The right brain is less field dependent than the left. *See* ROD AND FRAME TEST.

FRONTAL LOBE The front part of the cerebral cortex inside the forehead.

GLIOMA A brain tumor.

GNOSIA The perceptive ability that enables one to recognize things.

HEMI- Preceding a neurological symptom, "hemi" indicates that it affects only one side of the body.

HEMIDECORTICATION Hemispherectomy.

HEMISPHERE Half of the cerebral cortex. (See Figure 1, page 5.)

HEMISPHERECTOMY Surgical removal of half of the cerebral cortex.

HIPPOCAMPAL COMMISSURE A small bundle of nerves (near the hippocampus) connecting the left and right hemispheres. (See Figure 1, page 5.)

IDEATORY APRAXIA Inability to properly use objects.

IDEOMOTOR APRAXIA Inability to program complex movements. Simple automatic elements of movement may remain intact.

IPSILATERAL On the same side of the body (opposite of contralateral).

LATERALIZATION Left-right separation of function.

LESION An injury.

LIMBIC SYSTEM   The "smell brain." Intermediate in location and evolution between the "reptilian" brain and the cerebral cortex.

LONG-TERM MEMORY   Memory used in long-term recall as opposed to short-term memory used in the thinking process.

METAMORPHOPSIAS   A mental symptom in which objects appear distorted.

MOTOR SKILL   Skill in movement.

MYELINATION   A maturation process required before neurons can function.

NEOCORTEX   Cerebral cortex.

NEURON   The basic elements of brain and nerve tissue.

OCCIPITAL LOBE   The portion of the cerebral cortex under the back of the skull.

OLFACTORY   Relating to the sense of smell.

p   Statistical probability of experimental result occurring by chance.

PARAPHASIAS   Substitution of one word for another. A common symptom of aphasia.

PARIETAL   The middle portion of the cerebral cortex.

PLASTICITY   The ability to easily change form or organization. An infant's brain has so much plasticity that it can reorganize with speech in the right hemisphere if the left hemisphere is damaged.

PRAXIS   Control of manual activity.

PRIMARY PROCESS   Freudian term for the nonverbal, holistic thinking of the right brain.

PRIMATE   The order of mammals that includes apes, monkeys, and man.

PYRAMIDAL TRACT The neural connections between each hemisphere and the spinal cord.

RAVEN'S PROGRESSIVE MATRICES A test of logic and spatial ability used together.

REM (rapid eye movement) During sleep the periods of dreaming are associated by rapid movement of the eye muscles.

REPTILIAN BRAIN The most ancient part of the forebrain which sits on top of the brainstem.

RHINENCEPHELON Smell brain, limbic system.

RIGHT BRAIN The right hemisphere. Generally organized for nonverbal thinking in about 95 per cent of the population.

ROD AND FRAME TEST A measure of field dependence in which the subject tries to adjust an illuminated rod to the vertical position in a darkened room. The rod is surrounded by an illuminated square which is tilted by the examiner.

SEIZURE An epileptic attack. *See* EPILEPSY.

SET A mental "set" is a preconceived idea of how to solve a problem. Field-dependent, uncreative people have difficulty "breaking set."

SHORT-TERM MEMORY The memory process used in thought. Normally only important results are converted into long-term memory for later recall.

SINISTRAL Left-handed.

SMELL BRAIN The limbic system. First developed in evolution on smell-oriented nocturnal animals.

SOMATAGNOSIA Inability to identify parts of the body.

SOMATIC Relating to the soma or trunk. The body.

SPATIAL   Related to visualization and manipulation of objects in space. For example, perspective drawing and jigsaw puzzles require spatial ability.

SPLIT-BRAIN OPERATION   A commissurotomy.

STANFORD-BINET   The classic IQ test, which is losing ground to the Wechsler and other newer intelligence tests.

STREET FIGURES TEST   A test of ability to recognize figures represented by shadowy segments. Since only fragmented clues are available, it is an excellent test of the right-brain ability of "closure."

SYNERGY   A constructive partnership in which the whole is greater than the sum of its parts, e.g., man and computer.

TACHISTOSCOPE   A device for presenting visual material for only a fraction of a second. By having the subject look at a dot in the center, then flashing an image on one side or the other, a tachistoscope can be used to present images to only one hemisphere.

TEMPORAL LOBE   The portion of the cerebral cortex beneath the temples.

TRIUNE BRAIN   The idea of three evolutionary levels of the brain: the reptilian complex, the limbic system, and the neocortex.

WADA TEST   A test in which an anesthetic is injected in the artery feeding the left or the right hemisphere. By observing which functions are lost when a hemisphere is anesthetized, the functions handled by that hemisphere can be determined.

WAIS Wechsler Adult Intelligence Scale. An adult IQ battery of tests. *See also* WISC.

WECHSLER IQ *See* WAIS and WISC.

WERNICKE'S AREA An area in the lower rear of the left hemisphere important in associating language and thought.

WISC Wechsler Intelligence Scale for Children. A battery of twelve subtests—each with a maximum score of 20—is given. The subtests are as follows:

1. Information. Information from experience and education.

2. Comprehension. Practical knowledge and social judgment.

3. Arithmetic. Concentration and arithmetic reasoning.

4. Similarities. Logical and abstract thinking ability.

5. Vocabulary. Word knowledge from experience and education.

6. Digit Span. Attention and rote memory.

7. Picture Completion. Visual alertness and visual memory.

8. Picture Arrangement. Interpretation of social situations.

9. Block Design. Analysis and formation of abstract design.

10. Object Assembly. Putting together of concrete forms.

11. Coding. Speed of learning and writing symbols.
12. Mazes. Planning and following a visual pattern.

The first six tests are standardized by age and combined into a verbal IQ score indicating left-brain performance. The rest of the tests are standardized and combined into a performance IQ that measures right-brain performance. An IQ of 100 indicates average performance.

NOTES

1 YOUR SILENT PARTNER

1. While vision is completely separated down the center line, the center of the body has neural connections to both hemispheres. The left-right separation is more and more complete as we move away from the center of the body. Fingers thus have connections *only* to the opposite hemisphere, while arms are connected *primarily* to the opposite hemisphere. Appendix II summarizes the left-right neural "wiring."

2. Galin (1975). This experiment will be covered in more detail in Chapter 11.

3. Akelaitis (1944). Case histories of many of the patients are given. He concluded:

> Following complete section of the corpus callosum no disturbance in visual, auditory, and tactile gnosis [sensation] was observed and praxis [movement] and language functions were unimpaired.

4. Goldstein (1969), (1975). In both of these articles Dr. Goldstein follows up on the patients that Akelaitis had reported unchanged by their split-brain operation.

5. Gazzaniga (1978), p. 110. D.H.'s preoperative IQ scores were verbal 97, performance 86, while his postoperative scores were verbal 113, performance 90.

6. Ibid., p. 148.

7. Austin (1974), p. 103.

8. Akelaitis (1942).

2   THE "UNCONSCIOUS MIND"—DISCOVERED

David Galin originally presented many of the ideas in this chapter in an article in the *Archives of General Psychiatry* (Galin, 1974b).

1. Gardner (1974).

2. Risse (1976), p. 354. Also Gazzaniga (1978), pp. 14 and 131.

3. Galin (1974b). Also see p. 149 of Gazzaniga (1978) for a description of one split-brain patient's verbal rationalizations of his right hemisphere's responses.

4. Chandler (1977).

5. Buck (1976). Cohen (1976) found that eight of twelve subjects had strong peaks of EEG energy on the right side during orgasm.

6. Humphrey (1951).

7. Penfield (1959). Quotes given are on pages 35, 50, and 34, and in Penfield (1975).

8. Bakan (1976).

9. Bogen (1969b).

10. Austin (1971).
11. Cohen (1977).
12. Bakan (1976).

3 CREATIVITY AND THE RIGHT BRAIN

Bogen (1969c) was the source of many of the ideas in this chapter.

1. Golla (1929). Also Sokolov (1972) used electrical sensors to detect tongue movements during silent thought, reading, etc.
2. Haber (1970). The two subjects who viewed 1,280 slides a day for two days made 90 per cent and 89 per cent correct choices. The three subjects who viewed 640 slides a day for four days scored 95 per cent, 93 per cent, and 85 per cent. The four subjects who viewed the slides backward correctly chose 92 per cent, 94 per cent, 88 per cent, and 91 per cent while the four who were asked to tell whether the slides were backward or not scored 83 per cent, 91 per cent, 81 per cent, and 85 per cent.
3. Brooks (1968).
   The visual task required the subject to visualize a shape such as a block letter

and to examine mentally the corners one at a time in a clockwise sequence. At each corner he had to indicate by saying "yes" or "no" whether the corner was on the extreme top or bottom. If we start at the lower left corner of the letter above and proceed clockwise, we would answer "yes, yes, yes, no, no, no, no, no, no, yes."

The visual response consisted of indicating the same "yes" and "no" answers by underlining "Y"s and "N"s scattered randomly on a specially printed sheet. Since finding the scattered "Y"s and "N"s required visual thinking, the subjects found it difficult to keep track of where they were on the

$$\mathsf{F}$$

As long as they could think visually and report the answer verbally, there was no conflict, but doing two visual tasks at once was definitely conflicting.

When the problem was changed to a verbal problem, an opposite result was obtained: In this case the verbal response took *longer* than the visual. The verbal problem required holding a sentence in memory and indicating with a series of "yes" or "no" answers whether or not each word was a noun. With the verbal answering it became difficult to keep track of the words in the sentence while *saying* "yes" or "no." Locating the "Y"s and "N"s for the underlining (visual) response caused no such conflict because it used the separate visual thinking process.

The mean times (in seconds) for the four variations of the experiment are shown below:

	visual problem	verbal problem
visual response	28	9.7
verbal response	11	13

4. Hadamard (1945), p. 84.
5. Ibid., p. 142.
6. Wittrock (1975), p. 34.
7. Koestler (1964), p. 147.
8. Ibid., p. 212.
9. Hadamard (1945), p. 16.
10. Pearce (1974), p. 147.
11. Koestler (1964), p. 212. Collected the stories behind the "Eureka!" moment of illumination in many of the world's most important inventions. In each case the pattern is the same: a sudden *recognition* of a connection between the problem at hand and a seemingly unrelated principle or piece of knowledge.
12. Hadamard (1945), p. 30.

4 THE RIGHT-BRAIN REVOLUTION IN EDUCATION

1. Betts (1972) did a survey to determine the strength of various types of imagery for a large sample of people.
2. Mintzberg (1976).
3. Jex (1963), p. 239.

4. Ibid., p. 241.

5. Westcott (1963).

6. Whimbey (1976), p. 5.

7. Arnheim (1969), p. 221.

8. Franco (1977).

9. A third student with a congenital underdevelopment (agnesis) of the corpus callosum also had difficulty with geometry. He was also studied.

10. The scores given were actually for four types of geometry with progressively less constraints: Euclidean, affine, projective, and topological.

11. Olson (1977b).

12. Olson (1977a).

13. Olson (1977c), p. 9.

14. Beckman (1977).

15. Guilford (1968), p. 115.

16. Wittrock (1975), pp. 33 and 34.

17. Paivio (1971). The mean recall scores after five minutes and after one week for both learning conditions are tabulated below:

| | Intentional | | Incidental | |
	5 min.	1 week	5 min.	1 week
Pictures	33	19	36	16
Concrete nouns	24	10	14	8
Abstract nouns	14	5	11	2

18. Wechsler (1976), p. 191, did EEG studies which showed that when subjects were asked to think in words when recalling previously studied postcards, their right/left alpha ratio averaged 15 per cent higher

than when they recalled them as shapes and colors. When the subjects were asked to think in terms of *both* words and images, the alpha ratio was halfway between the two extremes. This confirms the theory that thinking in words tends to activate the left hemisphere, while thinking in images activates the right.

Also Sugishita (1978) showed that a split-brain patient (N.G.) could make coordinate, contingent, superordinate, and occupational associations with the right hemisphere but *abstract* associations were at chance level. Dichotic listening studies on normals by McFarland (1978) found that the mean number of word recognition errors with competing speech stimulus were as follows: abstract words 7.5 left ear, 3.6 right ear; concrete words 3.3 left ear, 5.3 right ear. Abstract nouns indeed seem to be a specialty of the left brain.

19. Bull (1973).
20. Schuster (1976).
21. Bever (1974). Also Johnson (1977).
22. Herrigel (1953).
23. Ibid.
24. Whimbey (1976), pp. 34 and 54.

5 THE INNER SPORTS REVOLUTION

1. Gallwey (1974), p. 25.
2. Lund (1976), (1977). Also Gallwey (1977b).

6 LATERALIZATION AND LANGUAGE PROBLEMS

1. Levy (1976), (1974a), (1977c).
2. Turkewitz (1977), pp. 310 and 313.
3. Molfese (1974), p. 361. Also (1977), p. 27.
4. Witelson (1977b).
5. Ibid., p. 250.
6. Fromkin (1974).
7. Neville (1977).
8. Witelson (1977a), p. 309.
9. Thomson (1976).
10. Bakker (1973).
11. Kershner (1977b). Different words were flashed on the left and right simultaneously after a fixation point was flashed at the center of the screen. R/L visual field accuracy scores were as follows: gifted readers 15/2.5, good readers 14/4, disabled readers 12/6. See also Marcel (1974).
12. Witelson (1977a). Conflicts between handedness, footedness, and eyedness were found in 65 per cent of dyslectics by Keeney (1968), p. 105. Side of hair whorl was also related to dyslexia by Tjossem (1962).
13. Simon (1977).
14. Whimbey (1976).
15. Wingate (1976), p. 93.

16. Hécaen (1964), p. 77.
17. Keeney (1968), p. 105. Also Hécaen (1964), p. 79.
18. Moore (1976).
19. Curry (1969).
20. Jones (1966). For a not too convincing attempt to relate "minimal brain damage" to laterality see Beaumont (1973).

7 SEX AND LEFT-HANDEDNESS

1. Rasmussen (1977).
2. Hécaen (1971). Bakan (1973b) found that 41 per cent of left-handers had stressful births as opposed to 22 per cent for right-handers. Some left-handedness may thus be a compensation for brain damage at birth. (This finding was not replicated by a later study.)
3. Levy (1977c).

The chart below shows the visual field difference scores for males and females of each of the four hand position types. Positive scores indicate a left-brain advantage for the task, while negative scores indicate right-brain superiority. RN (Right-hand non-inverted) and LI writers clearly have left-hemisphere (right visual field) language superiority, while RI and LN writers have language in the right brain. Notice also that field difference is strongest for noninverted males.

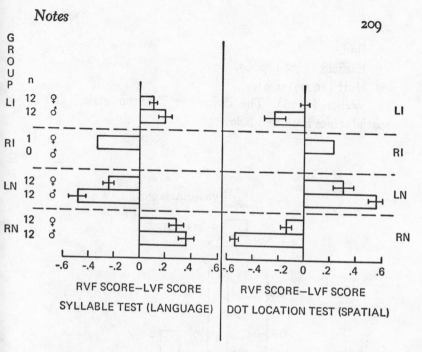

G
R
O
U
P

n

LI

RI

LN

RN

RVF SCORE—LVF SCORE
SYLLABLE TEST (LANGUAGE)

RVF SCORE—LVF SCORE
DOT LOCATION TEST (SPATIAL)

4. Hardyck (1977a). Jerre Levy should be given credit for originally developing this concept.

5. Hardyck (1976).

6. Sherman (1976). Subjects were given a list of thirty abstract and thirty concrete nouns to study. After they were distracted with a one-minute math problem, they were asked to recall as many nouns as possible. The results are tabulated below:

	Left-handed	Right-handed
Mean number of concrete nouns recalled	4.8	5.8
Mean number of abstract nouns recalled	4.6	4.3

7. Ibid.

8. Barfield (1976), p. 67.

9. Hutt (1972), p. 81.

10. Waber (1976). The difference between verbal and spatial scores is plotted below:

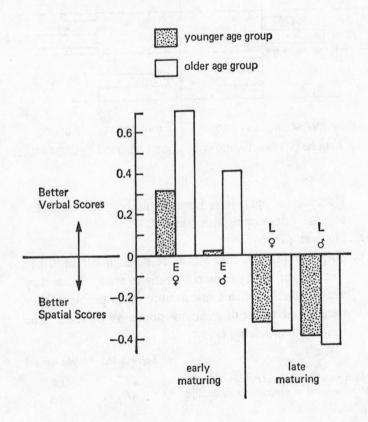

11. Maccoby (1974), pp. 75 and 94. Guilford (1967), p. 404.

12. Theilgaard (1972).

13. Netley (1977).

14. Kocel (1977). Also Maccoby (1974).

15. Wechsler (1944).

16. Guilford (1967), p. 404.

17. Lansdell (1962). Examples of other types of experiments showing sex differences are as follows: dichotic listening, Lake (1976); dot enumeration, McGlone (1973a); lateral eye movements, Gur (1974); EEG alpha ratio change, Tucker (1976). Levy (1977c) suggests that evolutionary survival advantage of woman's reduced lateralization is in her increased ability to do repetitive work without fatigue. The hemispheres can essentially "take turns" with a task.

18. McGlone (1978). This data was taken from Wechsler IQ testing of patients with unilateral brain damage at University Hospital, London, Ontario. The study also indicates that aphasic disorders were 3.7 times more common among males with left-brain damage.

19. Rizzolatti (1977). The L/R visual field reaction times at 1/50 sec. exposure were as follows: males .440/.595 seconds, females .550/.540 seconds.

20. Witelson (1976). Accuracy scores for visual recognition of nonsense shapes after simultaneously feeling a different shape with each hand are shown below. While

boys showed significantly more lateralization, total performance was virtually the same as that of the girls.

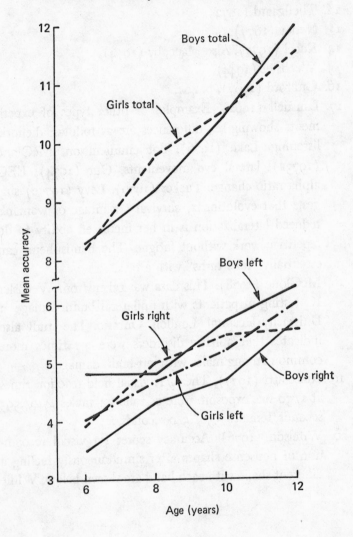

8 THE BRAIN IN THE COMPUTER AGE

1. Eccles (1977), p. 171.
2. Proc. IEEE, (1977).

9 THE SPLIT BRAIN

1. Sperry (1964).
2. Bogen (1962).
3. Sperry (1968b), p. 726.
4. Gazzaniga (1967). Both hemispheres have connections to the center of the body.
5. Sperry (1966).
6. Sperry (1968a), p. 318.
7. Ibid., p. 302. This is an excellent firsthand review of split-brain research in animals and humans. The surgical techniques of the operation are also discussed in easy terms.
8. Ledoux (1977) and Gazzaniga and Ledoux (1978), p. 110. The verbal portion of the WAIS IQ test increased from 97 to 113 and the performance score went from 86 to 90. The patient's score increased on 6 out of 7 subtests of the Wechsler memory test. His performance on a hypothesis learning test also improved. It is possible that these improvements may also be due to elimination of interference from the damaged portion of the right brain. Though Zaidel (1974) reported some short-term memory impairment after the split-

brain operation, it appears that this may have been the result of trauma from the surgical technique. D.H. and several other recent patients had their brains split by a new surgical technique which seems to have eliminated this problem.

9. Nebes (1971).

10. Nebes (1974), p. 159. The initials and per cent of right/left hand scores of the seven patients were as follows: A.A. 44/85, C.C. 30/70, N.G. 34/76, R.M. 43/89, N.W. 40/86, R.Y. 33/81, and L.B. 84/100. It was found that L.B.'s scores were nearly equal because he has incomplete separation of tactile sensation between hemispheres. Note that pure guessing among three choices would give an average score of 33.3 per cent.

11. Levy (1977b), p. 163.

12. Levy (1977a).

13. Zangwill (1974), p. 273.

14. Sperry (1968a), p. 318.

15. Ibid., pp. 310 and 319.

16. Sugishita (1978). Found that a split-brain patient (N.G.) could make four of five types of associations. After, for example, feeling a plastic spoon she could choose "fork" (coordinate association), "soup" (contingent), "silverware" (superordinate), and "cook" (occupation) from lists of similar words. She could *not*, however, make an *abstract* association. She guessed "truth" rather than "nutrition" as the abstract word most associated with the spoon.

17. Zaidel (1976).

18. The picture vocabulary tests used were the Peabody

and Ammon tests. The third subject, a thirteen-year-old with her left hemisphere surgically removed, had mental age scores of eight and ten years on the picture vocabulary tests and a Token test score below the three-year-old level.

19. Zaidel (1977). The patient is given a collection of small plastic "tokens" which he manipulates according to dictated instructions.

20. Gazzaniga (1970), p. 121.

21. Zaidel (1976), p. 202. Also see Zaidel (1977) for a more thorough discussion of the Token test.

22. Levy (1971).

23. Gazzaniga (1978), p. 143. The questions were asked verbally with a key word left blank; then the key word was flashed to the left visual field only. The rich language representation in P.S.'s right brain may be the result of early damage to the left hemisphere. It would be interesting to test the possibility that Ouija board responses could sometimes be responses of the right brain freed of left-brain inhibition.

24. Gordon (1969), p. 118. While complete separation of most smells from the left and right nostrils was found, certain emotional utterances seemed to have been initiated by the right brain.

An interesting discussion of why two consciousnesses can feel like one can be found in Puccetti (1977). Another discussion showing that consciousness and "self" are just fictional concepts can be found in Hebb (1967).

Chapter 7 of Gazzaniga (1978) relates some more

interesting split-brain experiments done at Dartmouth. He also suggests that our brain may have more than two conscious entities—we may be "a conglomeration of selves" (p. 161).

10 THE DAMAGED BRAIN

The Japanese have a phonetic alphabet (kana) and a pictorial language (kanja); aphasic patients often lose one and retain the other. See Geschwind (1972), Sasanuma (1975), and Sasanuma (1977).

1. Brown (1972), p. 151.
2. Gardner (1974), p. 354. See also De Renzi (1977).
3. Hécaen (1964). Reproduced in Appendix I.
4. Gardner (1974), p. 296.
5. Heilman (1975). See also Scholes (1975) and Gardner (1973).
6. Gainotti (1972).
7. Sperry (1967), p. 721.
8. Gardner (1974), p. 114.
9. Geschwind (1962).
10. Bogen (1969a). Shows many more examples of split-brain drawings. Also p. 241 of Pribram (1971) and p. 62 of Nielson (1946) relate to motor control.
11. Smith (1975). Describes the complete case history and gives scores on a complete battery of neurological tests.
12. Smith (1974), p. 10.
13. Ibid., p. 28.
14. Smith (1974), p. 20.
15. Kinsbourne (1974). The complete scores on a battery of neuropsychological tests are summarized below for

five adult hemispherectomy patients. These tests were given anywhere from ten days to thirty years after the operation. The four patients who had had their right brain removed all scored in the normal range in the verbal IQ, arithmetic, information, comprehension, and auditory retention tests. All four likewise did poorly on all of the nonlanguage tests requiring visual, spatial, and constructional abilities. These, of course, are the abilities that would have been best handled by their missing right brain. While the verbal IQ's of the four left brains were 99, 85, 99, and 103, their performance (nonverbal) IQ's were only 77, 63, 73, and 68.

16. Gardner (1955), p. 501.
17. Austin (1974), p. 105.
18. Bell (1949).
19. Smith (1966).
20. Ibid., p. 469.
21. Gott (1973a). Gives the complete case history and examines the pattern of language deficiency in this patient. Gott (1973b) compares this patient to two right-hemispherectomy patients. Hillier (1954). Gives a complete case history, but no quantitative test data.
22. Sutherland (1969).
23. Ibid., p. 1059.
24. Deglin (1976).
25. Ibid., p. 10.
26. Rasmussen (1977). Has an excellent description of the Wada procedure.
27. Gordon (1974a), p. 730.
28. Kinsbourne (1974), p. 264, and Trevarthen (1974), p. 190.

TABLE 4
RIGHT AND LEFT HEMISPHERECTOMY FOR BRAIN TUMOURS

	Right				Left		
	R1(GE)	R2(DB)	R3(JP)	R4(JH)		L1(EC)	
Postop Interval	1 yr.	15 yrs.	30 yrs.	10 days	10 mos.	19 mos.	20 mos.*
Age/Education (Years)	29/15	44/9	66/11	48/12	—	—	—
	Raw/Weighted Score		(WAIS)	(WBI)		(WAIS)	
Information	17/11	13/9	17/11	14/10	—	—	—
Comprehension	21/13	13/7	13/7	12/11	—	—	—
Arithmetic	7/7	8/7	9/8	6/7	12/11	1/1	3/3
Similarities	13/10	12/9	9/8	8/7	—	—	—
Digit Span	10/9	8/6	10/9	10/7	(6/2)	0/0	0/0
Vocabulary	—	24/7	40/10	27½/13	—	—	—
Digit Symbol	29/6	3/0	0/0	0/0	3/0	0/0	0/0
Picture Completion	9/7	7/6	4/4	5/3	14/10	14/10	4/4
Block Design	18/6	8/3	8/3	3/3	36/11	28/9	8/3
Picture Arrangement	16/7	10/5	10/5	0/0	20/9	24/10	0/0
Object Assembly	21/6	11/4	6/2	0/0	29/9	29/9	0/0
Verbal IQ	99	85	99	103	—	—	—
Performance IQ	77	63	73	68	110	108	56
Full Scale IQ	89	74	87	84	—	—	—
Peabody Picture Vocab.	125	95	109	—	98	91	—
Visual Memory	2	2	0	—	6	2	1
Copying Designs	10	4	5	—	10	—	0
Colored Matrices	18	8	14	—	32	27	18
Visual Organization	29	10½	7	—	29	22	—
SDMT Written	25	0	0	—	4	7	0
SDMT Oral	35	0	0	—	—	—	0
Porteus Maze	—	5½	6	—	15	14	—
DSS (Face-Hand)	normal	bilateral	bilateral	—	right sensory	right sensory	bilateral

* tumour reappeared

29. Lester (1977).

30. Ischlondsky (1955).

31. Friedland (1977), p. 2. Also Weinstein (1977) is a complete book dedicated to this symptom.

32. Friedland (1977), p. 11.
33. Battersby (1956).
34. Friedland (1977), p. 3.
35. Diller (1977), p. 79.
Many other interesting brain damage cases are described in Weinstein (1955).

11 THE NORMAL BRAIN

A detailed summary of the literature on hemispheric testing of normals is in Kimura (1973).

1. Jaynes (1976a).
2. Ibid., p. 120. Also see Bakan (1973a) and Nelson (1971).

Sackeim (1978) reported that the left side of the face seems to show emotion more strongly due to its more direct connection to the right brain. Composites of the two left sides of a photo of an emotional face (one printed in reverse) were compared to composites of the two right sides of the same photo. A group of eighty-five students rated the left side composites more emotional in eleven of the fourteen posers (people who posed for the photographs).

3. Pirozzolo (1977). Kershner (1972). The mean number of correct responses for L/R visual field were as follows: words 4.6/7.7, faces 6.7/3.6. The same right visual field preference for words was found in Chinese readers, so it does not appear to be related to left-right scanning habits.
4. Kimura (1974), p. 35.
5. Seamon (1974), p. 194. Left-hemisphere (right visual

field) reaction time increased from .535 seconds to .549 to .567 when the subject looked for one, two, and three words respectively. Right-hemisphere times were .522, .532, and .531 seconds.

6. Kimura (1973a), p. 78.
7. Kinsbourne (1977a), p. 178.
8. Entus (1977). The sucking rates gradually increased after the stimulus change to a peak at three minutes as follows: speech 85%/55% (right ear/left ear), music 53%/67%.
9. Galin (1975). This may sound backward unless we remember that *more* alpha indicates that a hemisphere is *idling*. For information on electrode locations see Doyle (1974); engineers vs. artists see Dumas (1975); EEG potentials evoked by flash and click see Davis (1977). Galin (1978) found that the change in alpha ratio increases as the task becomes more difficult.
10. Gur (1977a). Gross (1978). Found that intentional eye movements to one side or the other may tend to activate the opposite hemisphere. A test was given in which semantic or nonsemantic responses were possible. When the forty right-handed subjects intentionally looked left before answering, the mean number of nonsemantic responses was 2.5. When they looked right, the mean was only .8. Twenty left-handed subjects did the same test and had a mean of .7 nonsemantic responses for either direction of gaze.
11. Gur (1975a).
12. Gur (1975b). The scores of the left/bidirectional/right movers was 36%/42%/46% on the "turning against

object" rating. The "reversal" scores showed an opposite trend: 42%/35%/32%.

13. Schwartz (1975). The four question types used are listed below with an example of each followed by mean L/R eye movements:

1. Verbal—nonemotional: "What is the primary difference between the words 'recognize' and 'remember'?"   3.8/4.9

2. Spatial—nonemotional: "Imagine a rectangle. Draw a line from the upper left hand corner to the lower right hand corner. What two figures do you now see?"   4.3/3.1

3. Verbal—emotional: "For you is anger or hate a stronger emotion?"   4.9/3.7

4. Spatial—emotional: "When you visualize your father's face, what emotion first strikes you?"   5.1/2.4

14. Luria (1977).

15. Joynt (1977), p. 37. A review of medical literature proving lateralization from each of six different points of view can be found in McNeil (1974).

SELECTED
BIBLIOGRAPHY

The bibliography that follows lists only references that were found at least mildly novel or interesting. Articles that the author found particularly interesting are marked with an asterisk (*). Most articles listed should be available in any university medical library. The glossary should be helpful for readers who are not familiar with medical terminology.

Akelaitis, A. J., W. Risteen, R. Herren, and W. Van Wagenen. 1942. "Studies on the Corpus Callosum. III. A Contribution to the Study of Dyspraxia in Epileptics Following Partial and Complete Section of the Corpus Callosum." *Arch. Neurol. Psychiat.*, 47:971–1008.

Akelaitis, A. J. 1944. "A Study of Gnosis, Praxis and Language Following Section of the Corpus Callosum and Anterior Commissure." *J. Neurosurgery*, 1:94–102.

Albert, Martin L. 1973. "Simple Test of Visual Neglect." *Neurology*, 23:658–64.

Amheim, Rudolf. 1969. *Visual Thinking*. Berkeley: Univ. of California Press.

Austin, G., W. Hayward, and S. Rouhe. 1974. "A Note on the Problem of Conscious Man and Cerebral Disconnection by Hemispherectomy." In *Hemispheric Disconnection and Cerebral Function*. M. Kinsbourne and A. Smith, eds. Springfield, Ill.: Charles C. Thomas.

Austin, M. D. (*). 1971. "Dream Recall and the Bias of Intellectual Ability." *Nature*, 231:59–60.

Bakan, Paul. 1969. "Hypnotizability, Laterality of Eye-Movements and Functional Brain Asymmetry." *Perceptual and Motor Skills*, 28:927–32.

Bakan, Paul. 1976. "The Right Brain Is the Dreamer." *Psychology Today*, November 1976, pp. 66–68.

Bakker, D., T. Smink, and P. Reitsma. 1973. "Ear Dominance and Reading Ability." *Cortex*, 9:302–12.

Barfield, A. 1976. "Biological Influences on Sex Differences in Behavior." In *Sex Differences*, Michael S. Teitelbaum. Garden City, N.Y.: Anchor Press.

Basser, L. S. 1962. "Hemiplegia of Early Onset and the Faculty of Speech with Special Reference to the Effects of Hemispherectomy." *Brain*, 85:427–60.

Battersby, W., M. B. Bender, M. Pollack, and R. Kahn. 1956. "Unilateral 'Spatial Agnosia' ('Inattention') in Patients with Cerebral Lesions." *Brain*, 79:68–93.

Beaumont, J. Graham. 1974. "Handedness and Hemisphere Function." In *Hemisphere Function in the Human Brain*. S. Dimond and J. G. Beaumont, eds. New York: John Wiley.

Beaumont, J. G., and S. Dimond. 1975. "Interhemispheric Transfer of Figural Information in Right- and Non-Right-handed Subjects." *ACTA Psychologia*, 39:97–104.

Beaumont, J. G. 1976. "The Cerebral Laterality of 'Minimal Brain Damage' Children." *Cortex*, 12:373–82.

Beckman, Lucile (*). 1977. "The Use of the Block Design Sub Test of the WISC as an Identifying Instrument for Spatial Children." *Gifted Child Quarterly*, Spring 1977.

Bell, E., and L. M. Karnosh. 1949. "Cerebral Hemispherectomy: Report of a Case Ten Years After Operation." *J. Neurosurg.*, 6:285–93.

Bender, Morris B. 1977. "Extinction and Other Patterns of Sensory Interaction." In *Hemi-inattention and Hemisphere Specialization, Advances in Neurology*, Vol. 18. Weinstein and Friedland, eds. New York: Raven Press.

Bergan, A., D. McManis, and P. Melchert. 1971. "Effects of Social and Token Reinforcement on WISC Block Design Performance." *Perceptual and Motor Skills*, 32:871–80.

Betts, George H. 1972 (orig. 1909). *The Distribution and Functions of Mental Imagery*. New York: AMS Press.

Bever, T., and R. Chiarello. 1974. "Cerebral Dominance in Musicians and Nonmusicians." *Science*, 185:537–39.

Bisiach, Edoardo, Paolo Nichelli, and Hans Spinnler. 1976(a). "Hemispheric Functional Asymmetry in Visual Discrimination Between Univariate Stimuli: An Analysis of Sensitivity and Response Criterion." *Neuropsychologia*, 14:335–42.

Bisiach, Edoardo, and Erminio Capitani. 1976(b). "Cerebral Dominance and Visual Similarity Judgments." *Cortex*, 12:347–55.

Blakemore, Colin. 1977. *Mechanics of the Mind*. Cambridge: Cambridge Univ. Press.

Bogen, Joseph E., and P. S. Vogel. 1962. "Cerebral Commissurotomy in Man." *Bull. Los Angeles Neurol. Soc.*, 29:169–72.

Bogen, Joseph E. 1969(a). "The Other Side of the Brain I: Dysgraphia and Dyscopia Following Cerebral Commissurotomy." *Bull. Los Angeles Neurol. Soc.*, 34(2):73–105.

Bogen, Joseph E. 1969(b). "The Other Side of the Brain II: An Appositional Mind." *Bull. Los Angeles Neurol. Soc.*, 34(3):135–62.

Bogen, Joseph E., and Glenda M. Bogen (*). 1969(c). "The Other Side of the Brain III: The Corpus Callosum and Creativity." *Bull. Los Angeles Neurol. Soc.*, 34(4):191–217.

Bogen, J. E., R. DeZure, W. D. Tenhouten, and J. F. Marsh. 1972. "The Other Side of the Brain IV: The A/P Ratio." *Bull. Los Angeles Neurol. Soc.*, 37(2):49–61.

Bogen, Joseph E. 1975. "Educational Aspects of Hemispheric Specialization." *UCLA Educator*, 17(2):24 OUR (Spring 1975). Los Angeles: Univ. of California.

Boller, F., Y. Kim, and J. Mack. 1977. "Comprehension in Aphasia." In *Studies in Neurolinguistics*, Vol. 3. H. Whitaker and Whitaker, eds. New York: Academic Press.

Borlase, Jack. 1925. *The Ultimate Philosophy*. Salt Lake City: The Ultimate Philosophy.

Botkin, A., L. Schmaltz, and D. Lamb. 1977. " 'Overloading' the Left Hemisphere in Right-handed Subjects with Verbal and Motor Tasks." *Neuropsychologia*, 15:591–96.

Branch, C., B. Milner, and T. Rasmussen. 1964. "Intracarotid Sodium Amytal for the Lateralization of Cerebral Speech Dominance." *J. Neurosurgery*, 21:399–405.

Brandwein, P., and R. Ornstein. 1977. "The Duality of the Mind." *Instructor*, January 1977, pp. 54–58.

Brazier, M. A. 1962. "The Analysis of Brain Waves." *Scientific American*, June 1962.

Bremer, F. 1966. "Neurophysiological Correlates of Mental Unity." In *Brain and Conscious Experience*. John C. Eccles, ed. New York: Springer-Verlag.

Brooks, Lee R. (*). 1968. "Spatial and Verbal Components of the Act of Recall." *Canad. J. Psychol./Rev. Canad. Psychol.*, 22(5):349–68.

Broverman, D., E. Klaiber, Y. Kobayashi, and W. Vogel. 1968. "Roles of Activation and Inhibition in Sex Differences in Cognitive Abilities." *Psychological Review*, 75(1):23–50.

Brown, Jason W. 1972. *Aphasia, Apraxia and Agnosia*. Springfield, Ill.: Charles C. Thomas.

Brown, J., and J. Jaffe (*). 1975. "Hypothesis on Cerebral Dominance." *Neuropsychologia*, 13:107–10.

Bruce, Lewis C. (*). 1897. "Notes of a Case of Dual Brain Action." *Brain*, 18:54–65.

Bruner, Jerome S. 1973. *On Knowing*. New York: Atheneum.

Buck, Craig. 1976. "Knowing the Left from the Right." *Human Behavior*, June 1976, pp. 29–35.

Buckingham, H., and A. Kertesz. 1974. "Linguistic Analysis of Fluent Aphasia." *Brain and Language*, 1(1):43–62.

Buffery, A., and J. Gray. 1972. "Sex Differences in the Development of Spatial and Linguistic Skills." In *Gender Differences*. C. Ounsted and D. Taylor, eds. London: Churchill Livingstone.

Buffery, Anthony W. H. 1974. "Asymmetrical Lateralisation of Cerebral Functions and the Effects of Unilateral Brain Surgery in Epileptic Patients." In *Hemisphere Function in the Human Brain*. S. Dimond and J. G. Beaumont, eds. New York: John Wiley.

Bull, B., and M. Wittrock. 1973. "Imagery in the Learning of Verbal Definitions." *Brit. J. Ed. Psych.*, 43:289–93.

Calder, Nigel. 1970. *The Mind of Man*. New York: Viking Press.

Caramazza, A., J. Gordon, E. Zurif, and D. DeLuca. 1976. "Right-hemispheric Damage and Verbal Problem Solving Behavior." *Brain and Language*, 3:41–46.

Carmon, A., Y. Harishanu, E. Lowinger, and S. Lavy. 1972. "Asymmetries in Hemispheric Blood Volume and Cerebral Dominance." *Behavioral Biology*, 7:853–59 Abstract No. I-42R.

Carmon, A., I. Nachshon, and R. Starinsky. 1976. "Developmental Aspects of Visual Hemifield Differences in

Perception of Verbal Material." *Brain and Language,* 3:463–69.

Casasent, D., and D. Psaltis. 1977. "New Optical Transforms for Pattern Recognition." *Proceedings of the IEEE.* 65(1):77–83.

Chandler, B. C., and O. A. Parsons. 1977. "Altered Hemispheric Functioning Under Alcohol." *J. Studies on Alcohol,* 38(3):381–89.

Cohen, David B. 1977. "Changes in REM Dream Content During the Night: Implications for a Hypothesis About Changes in Cerebral Dominance Across REM Periods." *Perceptual and Motor Skills,* 44:1267–77.

Cohen, Gillian. 1973. "Hemispheric Differences in Serial Versus Parallel Processing." *J. Exper. Psych.,* 97(3):349–56.

Cohen, H., R. Rosen, and L. Goldstein. 1976. "Electroencephalographic Laterality Changes During Human Sexual Orgasm." *Arch. Sexual Behavior,* 5(3):189–99.

Cohn, Robert. 1977. "Symbol Retrieval Time as an Index of Attention." In *Hemi-inattention and Hemisphere Specialization, Advances in Neurology,* Vol. 18. Weinstein and Friedland, eds. New York: Raven Press.

Cole, R., and N. Cummings. 1977. "Bilateral Alpha Rhythm in Children During Listening and Looking." In *Language Development and Neurological Theory.* S. Segalowitz and F. Gruber, eds. New York: Academic Press.

Critchley, Macdonald. 1970. *The Dyslexic Child.* Springfield, Ill.: Charles C. Thomas.

Crockett, H. G., and N. M. Estridge. 1951. "Cerebral Hemispherectomy." *Bull. Los Angeles Neurol. Soc.*, 16:71–87.

Crovitz, Herbert F. 1962. "On Direction in Drawing a Person." *J. Consult. Psych.*, 26(2):196.

Curry, F., and H. Gregory. 1969. "The Performance of Stutterers on Dichotic Listening Tasks Thought to Reflect Cerebral Dominance." *J. Speech Hearing Research*, 12:73–82.

Dacey, Rob. 1975. "Inside the Brain: The Last Great Frontier." *Saturday Review*, August 9, 1975, p. 13.

Damasio, H., A. Damasio, A. Castro-Caldas, and J. M. Ferro. 1976. "Dichotic Listening Pattern in Relation to Interhemispheric Disconnexion." *Neuropsychologia*, 14:247–50.

Davis, A. E., and J. A. Wada. 1977. "Lateralisation of Speech Dominance by Spectral Analysis of Evoked Potentials." *J. Neurol. Neurosurg. and Psychiat.*, 40:1–4.

Davis, A., and J. Wada. 1978. "Speech Dominance and Handedness in the Normal Human." *Brain and Language*, 5:42–55.

Dawson, John, and L. M. Binnie. 1977. "An Anthropological Perspective on the Evolution and Lateralization of the Brain." *Annals New York Acad. Sci.*, 299:424–47.

Day, James. 1977. "Right-hemisphere Language Processing in Normal Right-handers." *J. Exper. Psych.: Human Percept. and Perform.*, 3(3):518–28.

Deglin, Vadim. 1976. "Split Brain." *The Unesco Courier,*
    January 1976, pp. 5–32.

Deikman, Arthur J. 1971. "Bimodal Consciousness." *Arch.*
    Gen. Psychiat., 25:481–89.

Dennis, Maureen, and Harry A. Whitaker. 1976. "Lan-
    guage Acquisition Following Hemidecortication: Lin-
    guistic Superiority of the Left over the Right Hemi-
    sphere." *Brain and Language,* 3:404–33.

Dennis, M., and H. Whitaker. 1977. "Hemispheric Equi-
    potentiality and Language Acquisition." In *Language*
    Development and Neurological Theory. S. Segalowitz
    and F. Gruber, eds. New York: Academic Press.

De Renzi, E., P. Faglioni, and P. Previdi. 1977. "Spatial
    Memory and Hemispheric Locus of Lesion." *Cortex,*
    13:124–29.

Diller, L., and J. Weinberg. 1977. "Hemi-inattention in
    Rehabilitation: The Evolution of a Rational Reme-
    diation Program." In *Hemi-inattention and Hemi-*
    sphere Specialization, Advances in Neurology, Vol.
    18. Weinstein and Friedland, eds. New York: Raven
    Press.

Dimond, S., and J. G. Beaumont. 1974. "Experimental
    Studies of Hemisphere Function in the Human
    Brain." In *Hemisphere Function in the Human Brain.*
    S. Dimond and J. G. Beaumont, eds. New York: John
    Wiley.

Dimond, S., L. Farrington, and P. Johnson (*). 1976.
    "Differing Emotional Response from Right and Left
    Hemispheres." *Nature,* 261:690–92.

Dimond, Stuart J. 1977(a). "Introductory Remarks."

Conference on the Evolution and Lateralization of the Brain. *Annals New York Acad. Sci.*, 299:1–3.

Dimond, Stuart. 1977(b). "Evolution and Lateralization of the Brain: Concluding Remarks." *Annals New York Acad. Sci.*, 299:477–99.

Doyle, J., R. Ornstein, and D. Galin (*). 1974. "Lateral Specialization of Cognitive Mode: II. EEG Frequency." *Psychophysiology*, 11(5):567–78.

Dreyer, A., E. Nebelkopf, and C. Dreyer. 1969. "Note Concerning Stability of Cognitive Style Measures in Young Children." *Perceptual and Motor Skills*, 28:933–34.

Dumas, R., and A. Morgan (*). 1975. "EEG Asymmetry as a Function of Occupation, Task and Task Difficulty." *Neuropsychologia*, 13:219–28.

Eccles, John C. 1977. "Evolution of the Brain in Relation to the Development of the Self-conscious Mind." *Annals New York Acad. Sci.*, 299:161–79.

Efron, Robert. 1963. "Temporal Perception, Aphasia and Déjà Vu." *Brain*, 86:403–24.

Entus, Anne K. (*). 1977. "Hemispheric Asymmetry in Processing of Dichotically Presented Speech and Nonspeech Stimuli by Infants." In *Language Development and Neurological Theory*. S. Segalowitz and F. Gruber, eds. New York: Academic Press.

Ettlinger, E. G., ed. 1965. *Functions of the Corpus Callosum*. Boston: Little, Brown.

Foster, Suzanne. 1977. "Hemisphere Dominance and the Art Process." *Art Education*, February 1977, pp. 28–29.

Friedland, R., and E. Weinstein. 1977. "Hemi-inattention and Hemisphere Specialization: Introduction and Historical Review." *Advances in Neurology*, Vol. 18. New York: Raven Press.

Friedman, J., J. Golomb, and M. Mora. 1952. "The Hair Whorl Sign for Handedness." *Diseases Nerv. Sys.*, July 1952, pp. 208–16.

Franco, Laura. 1977(a). "Hemispheric Interaction in the Processing of Concurrent Tasks in Commissurotomy Subjects." *Neuropsychologia*, 15:707–10.

Franco, L., and R. W. Sperry (*). 1977(b). "Hemisphere Lateralization for Cognitive Processing of Geometry." *Neuropsychologia*, 15:107–14.

Franklin, B., and P. Richards. 1977. "Effects on Children's Divergent Thinking Abilities of a Period of Direct Teaching for Divergent Production." *Brit. J. Ed. Psych.*, 47:66–70.

Fromkin, V., S. Krashen, S. Curtiss, D. Rigler, and M. Rigler. 1974. "The Development of Language in Genie: A Case of Language Acquisition Beyond the 'Critical Period.'" *Brain and Language*, 1(1):81–108.

Gainer, W. L. 1962. "The Ability of the WISC Subtests to Discriminate Between Boys and Girls of Average Intelligence." *Calif. J. Educ. Res.*, 13(1):9–16.

Gainotti, Guido. 1972. "Emotional Behavior and Hemispheric Side of the Lesion." *Cortex*, 8:41–55.

Galin, David, and Robert Ornstein. 1974(a). "Individual Differences in Cognitive Style—I. Reflective Eye Movements." *Neuropsychologia*, 12:367–76.

Galin, David. 1974(b). "Implications for Psychiatry of

Left and Right Cerebral Specialization." *Arch. Gen. Psychiatry*, 31:572–83.

Galin, D., and R. Ellis (*). 1975. "Asymmetry in Evoked Potentials as an Index of Lateralized Cognitive Processes: Relation to EEG Alpha Asymmetry." *Neuropsychologia*, 13:45–50.

Galin, David (*). 1977. "Lateral Specialization and Psychiatric Issues: Speculations on Development and the Evolution of Consciousness." *Annals New York Acad. Sci.*, 299:397–411.

Galin, David, J. Johnstone, and J. Herron. 1978. "Effects of Task Difficulty on EEG Measures of Cerebral Engagement." *Neuropsychologia*, 16:461–72.

Gallwey, W. Timothy. 1974. *The Inner Game of Tennis.* New York: Random House.

Gallwey, Timothy, and Bob Kriegel. 1977(a). *Inner Skiing.* New York: Random House.

Gallwey, Timothy. 1977(b). "This Man Can Change Your Skiing." *Ski*, January 1977, pp. 97–118.

Gardner, H., and G. Denes (*). 1973. "Connotative Judgements by Aphasic Patients on a Pictorial Adaptation of the Semantic Differential." *Cortex*, 9:183–96.

Gardner, Howard. 1974. *The Shattered Mind.* New York: Vintage Books.

Gardner, Howard. 1975. "Brain Damage: A Window on the Mind." *Saturday Review*, August 9, 1975, pp. 26–29.

Gardner, W. James, L. J. Karnosh, Christopher C. McClure, Jr., and Ann K. Gardner. 1955. "Residual

Function Following Hemispherectomy for Tumour and for Infantile Hemiplegia." *Brain*, 79:487–502.

Garrett, Susan V. 1976. "Putting Our Whole Brain to Use: A Fresh Look at the Creative Process." *J. Creat. Behav.*, 10(4):239–49.

Gazzaniga, Michael S. 1967. "The Split Brain in Man." *Brain and Consciousness*, August 1967, pp. 118–23.

Gazzaniga, Michael S. 1970. *The Bisected Brain*. New York: Appleton-Century-Crofts.

Gazzaniga, Michael S. (*). 1972. "One Brain—Two Minds?" *American Scientist*, May–June 1972, pp. 311–17.

Gazzaniga, Michael. 1974. "Cerebral Dominance Viewed as a Decision System." In *Hemisphere Function in the Human Brain*. S. Dimond and J. G. Beaumont, eds. New York: John Wiley.

Gazzaniga, Michael S. 1975. "Review of the Split Brain." *J. Neurology*, 209:75–79.

Gazzaniga, M. S. 1977. "Consistency and Diversity in Brain Organization." *Annals New York Acad. Sci.*, 299:415–23.

Gazzaniga, M., and J. LeDoux. 1978. *The Integrated Mind*. New York: Plenum Press.

Geffren, Gina. 1976. "Development of Hemispheric Specialization for Speech Perception." *Cortex*, 12:337–46.

Geschwind, Norman, and Edith Kaplan. 1962. "A Human Cerebral Deconnection Syndrome." *Neurology*, 12:675–85.

Geschwind, Norman. 1972. "Language and the Brain." *Scientific American*, April 1972.

Geschwind, Norman. 1974. "The Anatomical Basis of Hemispheric Differentiation." In *Hemisphere Function in the Human Brain*, S. Dimond and J. G. Beaumont, eds. New York: John Wiley.

Gilbert, Christopher. 1973(a). "Strength of Left-handedness and Facial Recognition Ability." *Cortex*, 9:145–51.

Gilbert, C., and P. Bakan (*). 1973(b). "Visual Asymmetry in Perception of Faces." *Neuropsychologia*, 11:355–62.

Goertzel, V., and M. G. Goertzel. 1962. *Cradles of Eminence*. Boston: Little, Brown.

Goldstein, Marvin N., and Robert J. Joynt. 1969. "Long-term Follow-up of a Callosal-sectioned Patient." *Arch. Neurol.*, 20:96–102.

Goldstein, Marvin N., Robert J. Joynt, and Ronald B. Hartley. 1975. "The Long-term Effects of Callosal Sectioning." *Arch. Neurol.*, 32:52–53.

Goleman, Daniel. 1977. "Split-Brain Psychology: Fad of the Year." *Psychology Today*, October 1977, pp. 89–90, 149–51.

Golla, F. L., and S. Antonovitch. 1929. "The Respiratory Rhythm in Its Relation to the Mechanism of Thought." *Brain*. 52:491–509.

Gordon, H. W., and R. W. Sperry. 1969. "Lateralization of Olfactory Perception in the Surgically Separated Hemispheres of Man." *Neuropsychologia*, 7:111–20.

Gordon, H. W., and J. E. Bogen. 1974(a). "Hemispheric Lateralization of Singing After Intracarotid Sodium Amylobarbitone." *J. Neurol. Neurosurg. Psychiat.*, 37:727–38.

Gordon, Harold W. 1974(b). "Auditory Specialization of the Right and Left Hemispheres." In *Hemispheric Disconnection and Cerebral Function.* M. Kinsbourne and A. Smith, eds. Springfield, Ill.: Charles C. Thomas.

Gott, Peggy S. (*). 1973(a). "Language After Dominant Hemispherectomy." *J. Neurol. Neurosurg. Psychiat.*, 36:1082–88.

Gott, Peggy S. 1973(b). "Cognitive Abilities Following Right and Left Hemispherectomy." *Cortex*, 9:266–73.

Green, E., and D. Howes. 1977. "The Nature of Conduction Aphasia." In *Studies in Neurolinguistics*, Vol. 3. H. Whitaker and Whitaker, eds. New York: Academic Press.

Greenberg, Al. 1977. "Mind over Skiing?" *Skiing*, 30(4):4–10.

Gross, Yigal, R. Franko, and I. Lewin. 1978. "Effects of Voluntary Eye Movements on Hemispheric Activity and Choice of Cognitive Mode." *Neuropsychologia*, 16:653–55.

Guilford, J. P., ed. 1947. *Printed Classification Tests.* Report No. 5, U. S. Army Air Force. U. S. Government Printing Office.

Guilford, J. P. 1967. *Nature of Human Intelligence.* New York: McGraw-Hill.

Guilford, J. P. 1968. *Intelligence, Creativity and Their Educational Implications.* San Diego: Robert Knapp.

Guilford, J. P. 1971. *The Analysis of Intelligence.* New York: McGraw-Hill.

Gur, R., and J. Reyher. 1973. "Relationship Between Style of Hypnotic Induction and Direction of Lateral Eye Movements." *J. Abnormal Psych.*, 82(3):499–505.

Gur, R. E., and R. C. Gur. 1974. "Handedness, Sex and Eyedness as Moderating Variables in the Relation Between Hypnotic Susceptibility and Functional Brain Asymmetry." *J. Abnormal Psych.*, 83(6):635–43.

Gur, R. E., R. C. Gur, and L. Harris (*). 1975(a). "Cerebral Activation, as Measured by Subjects' Lateral Eye Movements, Is Influenced by Experimenter Location." *Neuropsychologia*, 13:35–44.

Gur, R. E., and R. C. Gur. 1975(b). "Defense Mechanisms, Psychosomatic Symptomatology, and Conjugate Lateral Eye Movements." *J. Consult. and Clin. Psych.*, 43(3):416–20.

Gur, R. E., and R. C. Gur. 1977(a). "Correlates of Conjugate Lateral Eye Movements in Man." In *Lateralization in the Nervous System*. Harnad et al., eds. New York: Academic Press.

Gur, R. E., and R. C. Gur. 1977(b). "Sex Differences in the Relations Among Handedness. Sighting-Dominance and Eye-Acuity." *Neuropsychologia*, 15:585–90.

Haber, Ralph Norman. 1970. "How We Remember What We See." *Scientific American*, 222(5):104–12.

Hadamard, Jacques. 1945. *The Psychology of Invention in the Mathematical Field*. New York: Dover Publications.

Hamilton, Charles R. 1977. "An Assessment of Hemispheric Specialization in Monkeys." *Annals New York Acad. Sci.*, 299:222–32.

Hardyck, C., L. Petrinovich, and R. Goldman. 1976. "Left-handedness and Cognitive Deficit." *Cortex,* 12:266–79.

Hardyck, C. (*). 1977(a). "Individual Differences in Hemispheric Functioning." In *Studies in Neurolinguistics,* Vol. 3. H. Whitaker and Whitaker, eds. New York: Academic Press.

Hardyck, Curtis. 1977(b). "Handedness and Part-Whole Relationships: A Replication." *Cortex,* 13(2):177–83.

Hart, Leslie A. 1975. *How the Brain Works: A New Understanding of Human Learning, Emotion and Thinking.* New York: Basic Books, Inc.

Hatta, Takeshi. 1976. "Hemisphere Asymmetries in the Perception and Memory of Random Forms." *Psychologia,* 19(3):157–61.

Hebb, Donald O. 1967. "The Mind's Eye." In *Readings in Experimental Psychology Today.* Norman Adler, ed. Del Mar, Calif.: CRM Books.

Hécaen, H., and J. De Ajuriagueira. 1964. *Left-handedness: Manual Superiority and Cerebral Dominance,* trans. E. Ponder. New York: Grune & Stratton.

Hécaen, J., and J. Sauguet (*). 1971. "Cerebral Dominance in Left-handed Subjects." *Cortex,* 7:19–48.

Heilman, K. M., R. Scholes, and R. T. Watson. 1975. "Auditory Affective Agnosia." *J. Neurol. Neurosurg. Psychiat.,* 38:69–72.

Heilman, Kenneth M., and Robert T. Watson. 1977(a). "The Syndrome of Unilateral Neglect." In *Laterality in the Nervous System.* Harnard et al., eds. New York: Academic Press.

Heilman, K., and R. Watson. 1977(b). "Mechanisms Underlying the Unilateral Neglect Syndrome." In *Hemiinattention and Hemisphere Specialization, Advances in Neurology*, Vol. 18. Weinstein and Friedland, eds. New York: Raven Press.

Hellige, J., and P. Cox. 1976. "Effects of Concurrent Verbal Memory on Recognition of Stimuli from the Left and Right Visual Fields." *J. Exper. Psych.*, 2(2):210–21.

Hendricks, G., and R. Wills. 1975. *The Centering Book.* Englewood Cliffs, N.J.: Prentice-Hall.

Herrigel, Eugen. 1953. *Zen in the Art of Archery.* New York: Pantheon.

Herron, Jeannine. 1976. "Southpaws—How Different Are They?" *Psychology Today*, March 1976, pp. 50–56.

Hillier, William, Jr. 1954. "Total Left Cerebral Hemispherectomy for Malignant Glioma." *Neurology*, 4:718–21.

Holloway, Ralph L. 1976. "Paleoneurological Evidence for Language Origins." *Annals New York Acad. Sci.*, 280:330–48.

Humphrey, M. E., and O. L. Zangwill. 1951. "Cessation of Dreaming After Brain Injury." *J. Neurol. Neurosurg. Psychiat.*, 14:322–25.

Hunter, Madeline (*). 1977. "Right-brained Kids in Left-brained Schools." *The Education Digest*, February 1977, pp. 8–10.

Hutt, Corinne. 1972. "Neuroendocrinological, Behavioural, and Intellectual Aspects of Sexual Differentiation in Human Development." In *Gender*

Differences. C. Ounsted and D. Taylor, eds. London: Churchill Livingstone, pp. 73–122.

Ischlondsky, N. Dorin (*). 1955. "The Inhibitory Process in the Cerebrophysiological Laboratory and in the Clinic." *J. Nerv. Ment. Dis.*, 121:5–18.

Jaynes, Julian. 1976(a). *The Origin of Consciousness in the Breakdown of the Bicameral Mind.* Boston: Houghton Mifflin.

Jaynes, Julian. 1976(b). "The Evolution of Language in the Late Pleistocene." *Annals New York Acad. Sci.*, 280:312–25.

Jerison, Harry J. 1975. "Evolution of the Brain." *UCLA Educator.* 17(2):1 (Spring 1975). Los Angeles: University of California.

Jex, Frank B. 1963. "Negative Validities for Two Different Ingenuity Tests." In *Scientific Creativity: Its Recognition and Development.* C. Taylor and F. Barron, eds. New York: John Wiley.

Johnson, O., and A. Kozma. 1977. "Effects of Concurrent Verbal and Musical Tasks on a Unimanual Skill." *Cortex*, 13(1):11–16.

Johnson, Peter R. 1977. "Dichotically-Stimulated Ear Differences in Musicians and Nonmusicians." *Cortex*, 13:385–89.

Jones, R. K. (*). 1966. "Observations on Stammering After Localized Cerebral Injury." *J. Neurol. Neurosurg. Psychiat.*, 29:192–95.

Joynt, Robert J. 1977. "Inattention Syndromes in Split-Brain Man." In *Hemi-inattention and Hemisphere*

Specialization, *Advances in Neurology*, Vol. 18. Weinstein and Friedland, eds. New York: Raven Press.

Keeney, A. H., and Keeney, eds. 1968. *National Conference on Dyslexia, Philadelphia, 1966. Dyslexia—Diagnosis and Treatment of Reading Disorders*. St. Louis: Mosby.

Kershner, J., and A. Jeng. 1972. "Dual Functional Hemispheric Asymmetry in Visual Perception: Effects of Ocular Dominance and Postexposural Processes." *Neuropsychologia*, 10:437–45.

Kershner, John R. 1975. "Reading and Laterality Revisited." *J. Spec. Ed.*, 9(3):269–79.

Kershner, J., R. Thomas, and R. Callaway. 1977(a). "Nonverbal Fixation Control in Young Children Induces a Left-field Advantage in Digit Recall." *Neuropsychologia*, 15:569–76.

Kershner, John R. (*). 1977(b). "Cerebral Dominance in Disabled Readers, Good Readers, and Gifted Children: Search for a Valid Model." *Child Development*, 48:61–67.

Kertesz, Andrew, and Patricia McCabe. 1977. "Recovery Patterns and Prognosis in Aphasia." *Brain*, 100:60–75.

Kimura, Doreen. 1969. "Spatial Localization in Left and Right Visual Fields." *Canad. J. Psychol./Rev. Canad. Psychol.*, 23(6):445–58.

Kimura, Doreen. 1973(a). "The Asymmetry of the Human Brain." *Scientific American*, March 1973, pp. 70–78.

Selected Bibliography

Kimura, Doreen. 1973(b). "Manual Activity During Speaking—I. Right-handers." *Neuropsychologia,* 11:45–50.

Kimura, D., and M. Durnford. 1974. "Normal Studies on the Function of the Right Hemisphere in Vision." In *Hemisphere Function in the Human Brain.* S. Dimond and J. G. Beaumont, eds. New York: John Wiley.

Kimura, Doreen. 1977. "The Neural Basis of Language qua Gesture." In *Studies in Neurolinguistics,* Vol. 2. H. Whitaker and Whitaker, eds. New York: Academic Press.

Kinsbourne, Marcel. 1971. "The Minor Cerebral Hemisphere as a Source of Aphasic Speech." *Arch. Neurol.,* 25:302–6.

Kinsbourne, M. 1974(a). "Mechanisms of Hemispheric Interaction in Man." In *Hemispheric Disconnection and Cerebral Function.* M. Kinsbourne and A. Smith, eds. Springfield, Ill.: Charles C. Thomas.

Kinsbourne, M. 1974(b). "Lateral Interactions in the Brain." In *Hemispheric Disconnection and Cerebral Function.* M. Kinsbourne and A. Smith, eds. Springfield, Ill.: Charles C. Thomas.

Kinsbourne, M. 1974(c). "Cerebral Control and Mental Evolution." In *Hemispheric Disconnection and Cerebral Function.* M. Kinsbourne and A. Smith, eds. Springfield, Ill.: Charles C. Thomas.

Kinsbourne, M., and M. Hiscock (*). 1977(a). "Does Cerebral Dominance Develop?" In *Language Devel-*

opment and Neurological Theory. S. Segalowitz and F. Gruber, eds. New York: Academic Press.

Kinsbourne, Marcel. 1977(b). "Hemi-Neglect and Hemisphere Rivalry." In *Hemi-inattention and Hemisphere Specialization, Advances in Neurology,* Vol. 18. Weinstein and Friedland, eds. New York: Raven Press.

Kiparsky, Paul. 1976. "Historical Linguistics and the Origin of Language." *Annals New York Acad. Sci.,* 280:97–103.

Kocel, Katherine M. 1977. "Cognitive Abilities: Handedness, Familial Sinistrality, and Sex." *Annals New York Acad. Sci.,* 299:233–43.

Koestler, Arthur. 1964. *The Act of Creation.* New York: Dell.

Kohn, B., and M. Dennis. 1974. "Patterns of Hemispheric Specialization After Hemidecortication for Infantile Hemiplegia." In *Hemispheric Disconnection and Cerebral Function.* M. Kinsbourne and A. Smith, eds. Springfield, Ill.: Charles C. Thomas.

Krashen, Stephen D. 1973. "Lateralization, Language Learning, and the Critical Period: Some New Evidence." *Language Learning,* 23(1):63–74.

Krashen, Stephen D. 1975. "The Major Hemisphere." *UCLA Educator,* 17(2):17 (Spring 1975). Los Angeles: Univ. of California.

Krashen, Stephen D. 1977. "Cerebral Asymmetry." In *Studies in Neurolinguistics,* Vol. 2. H. Whitaker and Whitaker, eds. New York: Academic Press.

Lake, D., and M. Bryden. 1976. "Handedness and Sex Differences in Hemispheric Asymmetry." *Brain and Language*, 3:266–82.

Lang, Theodore. 1971. *The Difference Between a Man and a Woman*. New York: John Day.

Lansdell, H. (*). 1962. "A Sex Difference in Effect of Temporal-Lobe Neurosurgery on Design Preference." *Nature*, 194(4831):852–54.

Lansdell, H. 1964. "Sex Differences in Hemispheric Asymmetries of the Human Brain." *Nature*, 203(4944):550.

Ledoux, Joseph E., Gail L. Risse, Sally P. Springer, Donald H. Wilson, and M. S. Gazzaniga (*). 1977. "Cognition and Commissurotomy." *Brain*, 100:87–104.

Lee, P., R. Ornstein, D. Galin, A. Deikman, and C. Tart. 1976. *Symposium on Consciousness*. New York: Viking Press.

LeMay, Marjorie. 1976. "Morphological Cerebral Asymmetries of Modern Man, Fossil Man, and Nonhuman Primate." *Annals New York Acad. Sci.*, 280:349–66.

Leonard, George B. 1968. *Education and Ecstasy*. New York: Dell.

Leonard, George. 1974. *The Ultimate Athlete*. New York: Viking Press.

Lester, David. 1977. "Multiple Personality: A Review." *Psychology*, 14(1):54–59.

Levy, Jerre. 1969. "Possible Basis for the Evolution of Lateral Specialization of the Human Brain." 224:614–15.

Levy, Jerre, Robert D. Nebes, and Roger W. Sperry. 1971. "Expressive Language in the Surgically Separated Minor Hemisphere." *Cortex*, 7:49–58.

Levy, Jerre. 1974(a). "Psychobiological Implications of Bilateral Asymmetry." In *Hemisphere Function in the Human Brain*. S. Dimond and J. G. Beaumont, eds. New York: John Wiley.

Levy, Jerre. 1974(b). "Cerebral Asymmetries as Manifested in Split-Brain Man." In *Hemispheric Disconnection and Cerebral Function*. M. Kinsbourne and A. Smith, eds. Springfield, Ill.: Charles C. Thomas.

Levy, Jerre. 1976(a). "Evolution of Language Lateralization and Cognitive Effects." *Annals New York Acad. Sci.*, 280:810–19.

Levy, Jerre. 1976(b). "Lateral Dominance and Aesthetic Preference." *Neuropsychologia*, 14:431–45.

Levy, Jerre. 1977(a). "Manifestations and Implications of Shifting Hemi-inattention in Commissurotomy Patients." In *Hemi-inattention and Hemisphere Specialization, Advances in Neurology*, Vol. 18. Weinstein and Friedland, eds. New York: Raven Press.

Levy, Jerre, and Colwyn Trevarthen (*). 1977(b). "Perceptual, Semantic and Phonetic Aspects of Elementary Language Processes in Split-Brain Patients." *Brain*, 100:105–18.

Levy, Jerre. 1977(c). "The Mammalian Brain and the Adaptive Advantage of Cerebral Asymmetry." *Annals New York Acad. Sci.*, 299:264–72.

Levy, J. 1977(d). "Cerebral Asymmetries Preceding Speech." In *Studies in Neurolinguistics*, Vol. 3. H. Whitaker and Whitaker, eds. New York: Academic Press.

Lieberman, P., E. Crelin, and D. Klatt. 1972. "Phonetic

Ability and Related Anatomy of the Newborn and Adult Human, Neanderthal Man, and the Chimpanzee." *American Anthropologist*, 74:287–307.

Lomas, J., and D. Kimura. 1976. "Intrahemispheric Interaction Between Speaking and Sequential Manual Activity." *Neuropsychologia*, 14:23–33.

Lund, Morten. 1976. "Inner Skier: Will It Help You?" *Ski*, October 1976, pp. 101–3, 148–51.

Lund, Morten. 1977. "Inner Skier Meets the Skeptics." *Ski*, December 1977, pp. 97–99, 127.

Luria, A. R., and E. G. Simernitskaya. 1977. "Interhemispheric Relations and the Functions of the Minor Hemisphere." *Neuropsychologia*, 15:175–78.

Maccoby, Eleanor E. 1966. *The Development of Sex Differences*. Stanford, Calif.: Stanford Univ. Press.

Maccoby, E., and C. Jacklin. 1974. *The Psychology of Sex Differences*. Stanford, Calif.: Stanford Univ. Press.

McFarland, K., M. L. McFarland, J. D. Bain, and R. Ashton. 1978. "Ear Differences of Abstract and Concrete Word Recognition." *Neuropsychologia*, 16:555–61.

McGlone, J., and W. Davidson (*). 1973(a). "The Relation Between Cerebral Speech Laterality and Spatial Ability with Special Reference to Sex and Hand Preference." *Neuropsychologia*, 11:105–13.

McGlone, J., and A. Kertesz. 1973(b). "Sex Differences in Cerebral Processing of Visuospatial Tasks." *Cortex*, 9:313–20.

McGlone, Jeannette. 1978. "Sex Differences in Functional Brain Asymmetry." *Cortex*, 14:122–28.

McKee, Tim. 1977. "New Ways to Learn." *Ski*, October 1977, pp. 60–67.

McKim, Robert (*). 1972. *Experiences in Visual Thinking*. Monterey, Calif.: Brooks/Cole Pub.

McNeil, Malcolm R., and C. E. Hamre (*). 1974. "A Review of Measures of Lateralized Cerebral Hemispheric Functions." *J. Learning Disabilities*, 7(6):51–59.

Marcel, T., L. Katz, and M. Smith. 1974. "Laterality and Reading Proficiency." *Neuropsychologia*, 12:131–39.

Marshall, John C. 1973. "Some Problems and Paradoxes Associated with Recent Accounts of Hemispheric Specialization." *Neuropsychologia*, 11:463–70.

Marshall, J., and F. Newcombe. 1977. "Variability and Constraint in Acquired Dyslexia." In *Studies in Neurolinguistics*, Vol. 3. H. Whitaker and Whitaker, eds. New York: Academic Press.

Mensh, Ivan N., Henry G. Schwartz, R. G. Matarazzo, and J. D. Matarazzo. 1952. "Psychological Functioning Following Cerebral Hemispherectomy in Man." *Arch. Neurol. Psychiat.*, 67:787–96.

Miller, Edgar. 1971. "Handedness and the Pattern of Human Ability." *Br. J. Psychol.*, 62(1):111–12.

Mintzberg, Henry. 1976. "Planning on the Left Side and Managing on the Right." *Harvard Business Review*, July–August 1976, pp. 49–58.

Molfese, D., R. Freeman, and D. Palermo. 1974. "The Ontogeny of Brain Lateralization for Speech and Nonspeech Stimuli." *Brain and Language*, 1(4):356–67.

Molfese, D., V. Nunez, S. Seibert, and N. Ramanaiah. 1976. "Cerebral Asymmetry: Changes in Factors Affecting Its Development." *Annals New York Acad. Sci.*, 280:821–33.

Molfese, Dennis L. 1977. "Infant Cerebral Asymmetry." In *Language Development and Neurological Theory*. S. Segalowitz and F. Gruber, eds. New York: Academic Press.

Montagu, Ashley. 1967. "Chromosomes and Crime." In *Readings in Experimental Psychology Today*. Norman Adler, ed. Del Mar, Calif.: CRM Books.

Montagu, Ashley. 1976. "Toolmaking, Hunting, and the Origin of Language." *Annals New York Acad. Sci.*, 280:266–74.

Mooney, Ross L., and Taher A. Razik, eds. 1967. *Explorations in Creativity*. New York: Harper & Row.

Moore, W. H., Jr. (*). 1976. "Bilateral Tachistoscopic Word Perception of Stutterers and Normal Subjects." *Brain and Language*, 3:434–42.

Morais, Jose, and Michele Landercy. 1977. "Listening to Speech While Retaining Music: What Happens to the Right-ear Advantage?" *Brain and Language*, 4:295–308.

Moscovitch, Morris. 1977. "The Development of Lateralization of Language Functions and Its Relation to Cognitive and Linguistic Development: A Review and Some Theoretical Speculations." In *Language Development and Neurological Theory*. S. Segalowitz and F. Gruber, eds. New York: Academic Press.

Myers, Ronald E. 1976. "Comparative Neurology of Vocalization and Speech: Proof of a Dichotomy." *Annals New York Acad. Sci.*, 280:745–57.

Nash, John. 1970. *Developmental Psychology: A Psychobiological Approach*. Englewood Cliffs, N.J.: Prentice-Hall.

Nebes, Robert D. (*). 1971. "Superiority of the Minor Hemisphere in Commissurotomized Man for the Perception of Part-Whole Relations." *Cortex*, 7:333–49.

Nebes, Robert D. 1974. "Dominance of the Minor Hemisphere in Commissurotomized Man for the Perception of Part-Whole Relationships." In *Hemispheric Disconnection and Cerebral Function*. M. Kinsbourne and A. Smith, eds. Springfield, Ill.: Charles C. Thomas.

Nebes, Robert D. 1975. "Man's So-called 'Minor' Hemisphere." *UCLA Educator*, 17(2):13 (Spring 1975). Los Angeles: Univ. of California.

Nelson, T., and G. MacDonald. 1971. "Lateral Organization, Perceived Depth and Title Preference in Pictures." *Perceptual and Motor Skills*, 33:983–86.

Netley, C. (*). 1977. "Dichotic Listening of Callosal Agenesis and Turner's Syndrome Patients." In *Language Development and Neurological Theory*. S. Segalowitz and F. Gruber, eds. New York: Academic Press.

Neville, Helen. 1977. "Electroencephalographic Testing of Cerebral Specialization in Normal and Congenitally Deaf Children: A Preliminary Report." In *Language Development and Neurological Theory*. S. Segalowitz and F. Gruber, eds. New York: Academic Press.

Nielsen, J. M. 1946. *Agnosia, Apraxia, Aphasia*. 2nd ed. New York: Paul B. Hoeber.

Nottebohm, Fernando. 1970. "Ontogeny of Bird Song." *Science*, 167:950–56.

Olson, Meredith B. 1977(a). "Visual Field Usage as an Indicator of Right or Left Hemispheric Information

Selected Bibliography

Processing in Gifted Students." National Association for Gifted Children Convention, San Diego.

Olson, Meredith B. (*). 1977(b). "Right or Left Hemispheric Information Processing in Gifted Students." *The Gifted Child Quarterly*, 21(1):116–21.

Olson, Meredith B. (*). 1977(c). "Visual Field Usage as an Indicator of Right or Left Hemispheric Information Processing in Mathematically Precocious Students." Presented at the Annual Northwest Mathematics Conference, October 13, 1977, Seattle, Washington.

Oppenheimer, Jane M. 1977. "Studies of Brain Asymmetry: Historical Perspective." *Annals New York Acad. Sci.*, 299:4–17.

Ornstein, Robert E. 1972. *The Psychology of Consciousness*. San Francisco: W. H. Freeman.

Ounsted, C., and D. Taylor. 1972. "The Y Chromosome Message: A Point of View." In *Gender Differences*. C. Ounsted and D. Taylor, eds. London: Churchill Livingstone.

Paivio, Allen. 1971. *Imagery and Verbal Processes*. New York: Holt, Rinehart and Winston.

Paivio, Allen. 1975. "Imagery and Synchronic Thinking." *Canad. Psych. Rev.*, 16(3):147–61.

Paradis, M. 1977. "Bilingualism and Aphasia." In *Studies in Neurolinguistics*, Vol. 3. H. Whitaker and Whitaker, eds. New York: Academic Press.

Patterson, Francine G. 1978. "The Gestures of a Gorilla: Language Acquisition in Another Pongid." *Brain and Language*, 5:72–97.

Pearce, Joseph Chilton. 1974. *Exploring the Crack in the Cosmic Egg.* New York: Julian Press.

Pelletier, K., and C. Garfield. 1976. *Consciousness East and West.* New York: Harper & Row.

Penfield, W., and R. Lamar. 1959. *Speech and Brain Mechanisms.* Princeton, N.J.: Princeton Univ. Press.

Penfield, Wilder. 1975. *The Mystery of the Mind.* Princeton: Princeton Univ. Press.

Peterson, J., and L. Lansky. 1974. "Left-handedness Among Architects: Some Facts and Speculation." *Perceptual and Motor Skills,* 38:547–50.

Piaget, Jean. 1953. "How Children Form Mathematical Concepts." *Scientific American,* 189:74–79.

Piaget, Jean. 1973. *To Understand Is to Invent.* New York: Grossman.

Pines, Maya. 1966. *Revolution in Learning.* New York: Harper & Row.

Pines, Maya. 1973. *The Brain Changers.* New York: Signet.

Pirozzolo, F., and K. Rayner. 1977. "Hemispheric Specialization in Reading and Word Recognition." *Brain and Language,* 4:248–61.

Pizzamiglio, L., and M. Cecchini. 1971. "Development of the Hemispheric Dominance in Children from 5 to 10 Years of Age and Their Relations with the Development of Cognitive Processes." *Brain Research,* 31:361–78.

Pribram, Karl H. 1971. *Languages of the Brain.* Englewood Cliffs, N.J.: Prentice-Hall.

Pribram, Karl H. 1977. "Hemispheric Specialization: Evolution or Revolution." *Annals New York Acad. Sci.,* 299:18–21.

Puccetti, Roland (*). 1977. "Bilateral Organization of Consciousness in Man." *Annals New York Acad. Sci.,* 299:448–58.

Rasmussen, T., and B. Milner (*). 1977. "The Role of Early Left-brain Injury in Determining Lateralization of Cerebral Speech Functions." *Annals New York Acad. Sci.,* 280:355–69.

Ray, W., M. Morell, A. Frediani, and D. Tucker (*). 1976. "Sex Differences and Lateral Specialization of Hemispheric Functioning." *Neuropsychologia,* 14:391–94.

Regelski, Thomas A. (*). 1977. "Music Education and the Human Brain." *The Education Digest,* October 1977, pp. 44–47.

Rhodes, L., R. Dustman, and E. Beck (*). 1969. "The Visual Evoked Response: A Comparison of Bright and Dull Children." *Electroenceph. Clin. Neurophysiol.,* 27:364–72.

Risse, Gail L., and M. S. Gazzaniga. 1976. "Verbal Retrieval of Right Hemisphere Memories Established in the Absence of Language." Paper presented at meeting of the American Academy of Neurology, April 29, 1976.

Rizzolatti, G., and H. Buchtel (*). 1977. "Hemispheric Superiority in Reaction Time to Faces: A Sex Difference." *Cortex,* 13:300–5.

Robbins, K., and D. McAdam. 1974. "Interhemispheric Alpha Asymmetry and Imagery Mode." *Brain and Language*, 1:189–93.

Rose, Steven. 1976. *The Conscious Brain*. New York: Vintage Books.

Rosner, Stanley, and Lawrence Abt. 1970. *The Creative Experience*. New York: Grossman.

Rugg, Harold. 1963. *Imagination*. New York: Harper & Row.

Sackeim, Harold, and R. Gur. 1978. "Lateral Asymmetry in Intensity of Emotional Expression." *Neuropsychologia*, 16:473–81.

Sagan, Carl. 1977. *The Dragons of Eden*. New York: Random House.

Sage, Wayne. 1976. "The Split Brain Lab." *Human Behavior*, June 1976, pp. 25–28.

Samples, Robert E. 1975. "Are You Teaching Only One Side of the Brain?" *Learning*, February 1975, pp. 25–28.

Samples, Bob. 1977. "Mind Cycles and Learning." *Phi Delta Kappan*, May 1977, pp. 688–92.

Sasanuma, S., and H. Monoi. 1975. "The Syndrome of Gogi (Word-Meaning) Aphasia." 25:627–32.

Sasanuma, S., M. Itho, K. Mori, and Y. Kobayashi. 1977. "Tachistoscopic Recognition of Kana and Kanji Words." *Neuropsychologia*, 15:547–53.

Schain, Richard J. 1977. *Neurology of Childhood Learning Disorders*. Baltimore: Williams and Wilkins.

Schlanger, B., and P. Schlanger. 1976. "The Perception of

Emotionally Toned Sentences by Right Hemisphere-damaged and Aphasic Subjects." *Brain and Language*, 3:396–403.

Schuster, Benitz-Burdon, and C. Gritton. 1976. *Suggestive Accelerative Learning and Teaching: A Manual of Classroom Procedures Based on the Lozanov Method.* Des Moines, Iowa: Charles Gritton.

Schwartz, G., R. Davidson, and F. Maer (*). 1975. "Right Hemisphere Lateralization for Emotion in the Human Brain: Interactions with Cognition." *Science*, 190:286–88.

Seamon, John G. 1974. "Coding and Retrieval Processes and the Hemispheres of the Brain." In *Hemisphere Function in the Human Brain.* S. Dimond and J. G. Beaumont, eds. New York: John Wiley.

Segalowitz, S., and F. Gruber, eds. 1977. *Language Development and Neurological Theory.* New York: Academic Press.

Selnes, Ola Arvid. 1974. "The Corpus Callosum: Some Anatomical and Functional Considerations with Special Reference to Language." *Brain and Language*, 1(1):111–40.

Sherman, J., R. Kulhavy, and K. Burns (*). 1976. "Cerebral Laterality and Verbal Processes." *J. Exper. Psych.*, 2(6):720–27.

Shouksmith, George. 1970. *Intelligence, Creativity and Cognitive Style.* London: B. T. Batsford.

Silverman, A., G. Adevai, and W. McGough. 1966. "Some Relationships Between Handedness and Perception." *J. Psychosomatic Res.*, 10:151–58.

Simon, Debbie. 1977. "The Battle to Read." *Wall Street Journal*, October 13, 1977, pp. 1, 27.

Smith, Aaron. 1966. "Speech and Other Functions After Left (Dominant) Hemispherectomy." *J. Neurol. Neurosurg. Psychiat.*, 29:467–71.

Smith, Aaron. 1974. "Dominant and Nondominant Hemispherectomy." In *Hemispheric Disconnection and Cerebral Function*. M. Kinsbourne and A. Smith, eds. Springfield, Ill.: Charles C. Thomas.

Smith, Aaron, and Oscar Sugar (*). 1975(a). "Development of Above Normal Language and Intelligence 21 Years After Left Hemispherectomy." *Neurology*, 25:813–18.

Smith, Adam. 1975. *Powers of Mind*. New York: Random House.

Sokolov, A. N. 1972. *Inner Speech and Thought*. New York: Plenum Press.

Sperry, Roger W. 1962. "Some General Aspects of Interhemispheric Integration." *Interhemispheric Relations and Cerebral Dominance*. Conference. J. Young, ed. Baltimore: Johns Hopkins Univ. Press.

Sperry, R. W. (*). 1964. "The Great Cerebral Commissure." *Scientific American*, January 1964, pp. 42–52.

Sperry, Roger W. (*). 1966. "Brain Bisection and Mechanisms of Consciousness." In *Brain and Conscious Experience*. John C. Eccles, ed. New York: Springer-Verlag.

Sperry, R. W. 1967. "Split-Brain Approach to Learning Problems." In *The Neurosciences: A Study Program*.

G. C. Quarton, T. Melnechuk, and F. C. Schmitt, eds. New York: Rockefeller Univ. Press.

Sperry, R. W. 1968(a). "Mental Unity Following Surgical Disconnection of the Cerebral Hemispheres." Harvey Lectures, Series 62. New York: Academic Press.

Sperry, R. W. (*). 1968(b). "Hemisphere Deconnection and Unity in Conscious Awareness." *Amer. Psychologist*, 23:723–33.

Sperry, R. W. 1975. "Left Brain, Right Brain." *Saturday Review*, August 9, 1975, pp. 30–33.

Sperry, Roger. 1976. "Messages from the Laboratory." *Academic Therapy*, 11(2):149–55.

Springer, S., and M. Gazzaniga. 1975. "Dichotic Testing of Partial and Complete Split Brain Subjects." *Neuropsychologia*, 13:341–46.

Starck, R., F. Genesee, W. Lambert, and M. Seitz. 1977. "Multiple Language Experience and the Development of Cerebral Dominance." In *Language Development and Neurological Theory*. S. Segalowitz and F. Gruber, eds. New York: Academic Press.

Sugishita, Morihiro. 1978. "Mental Association in the Minor Hemisphere of a Commissurotomy Patient." *Neuropsychologia*, 16:229–32.

Sutherland, Edmond M., John E. Oliver, and Diana R. Knight. 1969. "E.E.G., Memory and Confusion in Dominant, Non-Dominant and Bi-Temporal E.C.T." *Br. J. Psychiat.*, 115:1059–64.

Sweeney, Edward J. 1953. *Sex Differences in Problem Solving*. Doctoral dissertation, Stanford University. 3781 S78 S974.

Szilak, Dennis. 1976. "Strings: A Critique of Systematic Education." *Harvard Educ. Rev.*, 46(1):54–75.

Taylor, Donald W. 1960. "Thinking and Creativity." *Annals New York Acad. Sci.*, 91:108–23.

Taylor, Donald W. 1963. "Variables Related to Creativity and Productivity." In *Scientific Creativity: Its Recognition and Development.* C. Taylor and F. Barron, eds. New York: John Wiley.

Theilgaard, Alice. 1972. "Cognitive Style and Gender Role in Persons with Sex Chromosome Aberrations." *Danish Medical Bull.*, 19(8):276–86.

Thomson, M. E. (*). 1976. "A Comparison of Laterality Effects in Dyslexics and Controls Using Verbal Dichotic Listening Tasks." *Neuropsychologia*, 14:243–46.

Tjossem, T., T. Hansen, and H. Ripley. 1962. "Investigation of Reading Difficulty in Young Children." *Amer. J. Psychiat.*, 118:1104–13.

Trevarthen, Colwyn. 1974(a). "Cerebral Embryology and the Split Brain." In *Hemispheric Disconnection and Cerebral Function.* M. Kinsbourne and A. Smith, eds. Springfield, Ill.: Charles C. Thomas.

Trevarthen, Colwyn. 1974(b). "Functional Relations of Disconnected Hemispheres with the Brain Stem, and with Each Other: Monkey and Man." In *Hemispheric Disconnection and Cerebral Function.* M. Kinsbourne and A. Smith, eds. Springfield, Ill.: Charles C. Thomas.

Tucker, D., R. Roth, B. Arneson, and V. Buckingham (*). 1977. "Right Hemisphere Activation During Stress." *Neuropsychologia*, 15:697–700.

Turkewitz, Gerald. 1977. "The Development of Lateral Differentiation in the Human Infant." *Annals New York Acad. Sci.*, 299:309–18.

Udell, G., K. Baker, and G. Albaum. 1976. "Creativity: Necessary, but Not Sufficient." *J. Creat. Behav.*, 10(3).

Van Riper, Charles (*). 1971. *The Nature of Stuttering*. Englewood Cliffs, N.J.: Prentice-Hall.

Virshup, Evelyn. 1976. "Art and the Right Hemisphere." *Art Education*, November 1976, pp. 14–15.

Waber, Deborah P. (*). 1976. "Sex Differences in Cognition: A Function of Maturation Rate?" *Science*, 192:572–73.

Wada, J., R. Clarke, and A. Hamm. 1975. "Cerebral Hemispheric Asymmetry in Humans." *Arch. Neurol.*, 32:239–45.

Wada, Juhn A. 1977. "Pre-Language and Fundamental Asymmetry of the Infant Brain." *Annals New York Acad. Sci.*, 299:370–79.

Walkup, Lewis E. 1965. "Creativity in Science Through Visualization." *Perceptual and Motor Skills*, 21:35–41.

Wallas, G. 1945. *The Art of Thought*. London: C. A. Watts.

Warren, J. M., and A. J. Nonneman. 1976. "The Search for Cerebral Dominance in Monkeys." *Annals New York Acad. Sci.*, 280:732–44.

Warren, J. M. 1977. "Functional Lateralization of the Brain." *Annals New York Acad. Sci.*, 299:273–80.

Webster, William G. 1977. "Territoriality and the Evolution of Brain Asymmetry." *Annals New York Acad. Sci.*, 299:213–21.

Wechsler, Adam F. 1976. "Crossed Aphasia in an Illiterate Dextral." *Brain and Language*, 3:164–72.

Wechsler, David. 1944. *The Measurement of Adult Intelligence.* Baltimore: Williams and Wilkins.

Weinstein, Ed. A., and R. L. Kahn (*). 1955. *Denial of Illness.* Springfield, Ill.: Charles C. Thomas.

Weinstein, E., and R. Friedland. 1977. "Concluding Remarks." In *Hemi-inattention and Hemisphere Specialization, Advances in Neurology*, Vol. 18. Weinstein and Friedland, eds. New York: Raven Press.

Westcott, M., and J. Ranzoni. 1963. "Correlates of Intuitive Thinking." *Psychological Reports*, 12:595–613.

Whimbey, A., with L. Whimbey. 1976. *Intelligence Can Be Taught.* New York: Bantam Books.

Whitaker, H., and G. Ojemann. 1977. "Lateralization of Higher Cortical Functions." *Annals New York Acad. Sci.*, 299:459–73.

Wingate, Marcel E. 1976. *Stuttering: Theory and Treatment.* New York: Irvington (Wiley).

Witelson, S., and M. Rabinovitch. 1972. "Hemispheric Speech Lateralization in Children with Auditory-Linguistic Deficits." *Cortex*, 8:412–26.

Witelson, Sandra (*). 1976. "Sex and the Single Hemisphere: Specialization of the Right Hemisphere for Spatial Processing." *Science*, 193:425–26.

Witelson, Sandra F. (*). 1977(a). "Developmental Dyslexia: Two Right Hemispheres and None Left." *Science*, 195:309–11.

Witelson, Sandra F. 1977(b). "Early Hemisphere Specialization and Interhemispheric Plasticity." In *Language Development and Neurological Theory*. S. Segalowitz and F. Gruber, eds. New York: Academic Press.

Witkin, H. A. 1949. "Sex Differences in Perception." *Transactions New York Acad. Sci.*, 12:22–26.

Witkin, H., R. Dyk, H. Faterson, D. Goodenough, and S. Karp. 1962. *Psychological Differentiation*. New York: John Wiley.

Wittrock, M. C. 1975. "The Generative Processes of Memory." *UCLA Educator*, 17(2):33 (Spring 1975). Los Angeles: Univ. of California.

Wolff, Peter H. 1977. "The Development of Manual Asymmetries in Motor Sequencing Skills." *Annals New York Acad. Sci.*, 299:319–27.

Wooldridge, Dean E. 1963. *The Machinery of the Brain*. New York: McGraw-Hill.

Young, Gerald. 1977. "Manual Specialization in Infancy: Implications for Lateralization of Brain Function." In *Language Development and Neurological Theory*. S. Segalowitz and F. Gruber, eds. New York: Academic Press.

Yukawa, Hideki. 1973. *Creativity and Intuition*. Tokyo: Kodansha International.

Zaidel, Dahlia, and R. W. Sperry. 1974. "Memory Impairment After Commissurotomy in Man." *Brain*, 97:263–72.

Zaidel, Dahlia, and Roger W. Sperry. 1977. "Some Long-term Motor Effects of Cerebral Commissurotomy in Man." *Neuropsychologia*, 15:193–204.

Zaidel, Eran. 1976. "Auditory Vocabulary of the Right Hemisphere Following Brain Bisection or Hemidecortication." *Cortex*, 12:191–211.

Zaidel, Eran. 1977. "Unilateral Auditory Language Comprehension on the Token Test Following Cerebral Commissurotomy and Hemispherectomy." *Neuropsychologia*, 15:1–18.

Zangwill, Oliver L. 1974. "Consciousness and the Cerebral Hemispheres." In *Hemisphere Function in the Human Brain*. S. Dimond and J. G. Beaumont, eds. New York: John Wiley.

INDEX

Index

Index